3

Zaner-Bloser
Handwriting

Teacher Edition

Zaner-Bloser, Inc.
P.O. Box 16764
Columbus, Ohio 43216-6764
800.421.3018
www.zaner-bloser.com

ISBN-13 978-0-7367-5154-4
ISBN-10 0-7367-5154-8

Printed in the United States of America

08 09 10 11 (330) 5 4 3 2

Grade 3 Teacher Edition
Table of Contents

Zaner-Bloser Handwriting

The Way to Write!

Proven Effective
Our classroom-tested methods have a long history of producing legible handwriting.

Committed to Handwriting Instruction
Our mission is to provide a full-spectrum of quality instructional materials that are easy to teach and implement.

Backed by Research
Our instructional materials are developed in accord with leading handwriting and educational researchers to best support beginning reading and writing instruction.

Meets the Needs of All Students
Our program delivers developmentally-appropriate instruction for students in PreK through Middle School and helps increase overall student achievement.

AaBbCc

Program Components

◀ **Student Edition**
- Easy step-by-step instruction
- Meaningful practice and application
- Colorful and fun

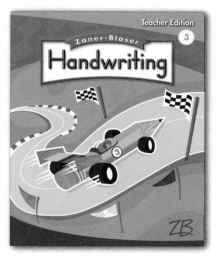

◀ **Teacher Edition**
- Full annotation
- Simple step-by-step guide
- Handy Evaluation Guide

Practice Masters ▶
- More practice for every letter and skill
- Additional resources include certificates, evaluation record, and school-to-home letters

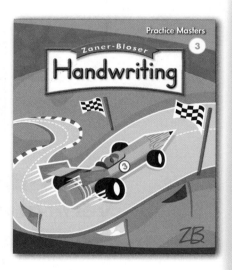

◀ **Poster/Wall Chart Super Pack**
A perfect addition to the handwriting classroom, includes:
- Manuscript and Cursive Alphabet Posters
- Keys to Legibility Poster
- Handwriting Positions Poster

Zaner-Bloser Handwriting

The Alphabets That Support Reading and Writing

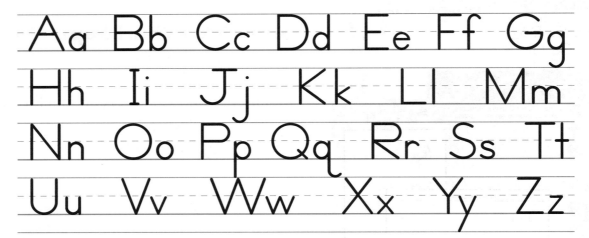

From Manuscript...

Zaner-Bloser's continuous-stroke, vertical manuscript alphabet

- Promotes automaticity because students only need to learn four simple strokes
- Reinforces reading because students see vertical manuscript everyday, inside and outside the classroom

Aa Bb Cc Dd Ee Ff Gg
Hh Ii Jj Kk Ll Mm
Nn Oo Pp Qq Rr Ss Tt
Uu Vv Ww Xx Yy Zz

...to Cursive.

Zaner-Bloser's simplified cursive alphabet

- Leads to legible cursive writing
- Helps students get higher test scores because, as legible cursive writing becomes automatic, students can focus more energy on their message

Aa Bb Cc Dd Ee Ff

Gg Hh Ii Jj Kk

Ll Mm Nn Oo Pp

Qq Rr Ss Tt Uu

Vv Ww Xx Yy Zz

Zaner-Bloser Handwriting provides options to begin cursive writing instruction in Grade 2 or Grade 3.

The Student Edition

Zaner-Bloser Handwriting guides students through an easy step-by-step process for learning good, legible handwriting that will last a lifetime.

Letter models with arrows show stroke sequence.

Shaded letters for tracing are provided.

Starting dots show students where to begin the letter.

Stop-and-Check signs remind students to evaluate their letters.

School-to-Home stroke descriptions help families reinforce and evaluate student handwriting at home.

Trace and write.

V ν   ν

five volleyballs on vacation
five volleyballs on vacation

Trace and write.

ν

Join ν and other letters. Notice the checkstroke to overcurve joining.

vy vi va ove ive ave

envy very visitor

School to Home
Stroke description to guide letter formation at home:
Overcurve; slant; undercurve.
Checkstroke.
ν

Slant
Circle a letter you wrote that has good slant.

70

Grade 3 student page

A **Practice** page in each section gives students another chance to practice and review.

Practice

n m y x v z

Write these color words.

maroon lime orange

neon green tangerine

violet lavender silver

yellow ivory azure

pink a color mix

Complete this sentence.
My favorite color is

72

Grade 3 student page

Z8

Writing practice is done directly beneath a model. This model provides a visual guide that both left- and right-handed students can easily see.

Trace and write.

z z z z z z z

amazing mazes
amazing mazes

Trace and write.

z z z z z z z z

Join z and other letters.

zy zi ze za ize oze

zebra zipper zigzag

School to Home Stroke description to guide letter formation at home:
z Overcurve; slant. Overcurve; curve down; loop; overcurve.

Slant
Circle a word you wrote that has good slant.

Grade 3 student page

71

Joinings provide students with practice connecting cursive letters.

The Key to Legibility prompts students to evaluate their handwriting.

Application

What a great day for a picnic!
Write these phrases that describe the picture.

marvelous gigantic salad

amazing icy lemonade

tasty turkey sandwiches

yummy yellow mustard

juicy melon

excellent pie

Keys to Legibility
My writing has good shape. ☐
My writing has good size. ☐
My writing has good spacing. ☐
My writing has good slant. ☐

73

Grade 3 student page

The **Application** page at the end of every section provides writing practice that

- Makes important connections to language arts and content areas
- Prompts students to evaluate their handwriting using the Keys to Legibility

The Way to Legibility

Four Keys to Legibility—**Shape, Size, Spacing,** and **Slant**—are the basis of Zaner-Bloser's unique instructional system.

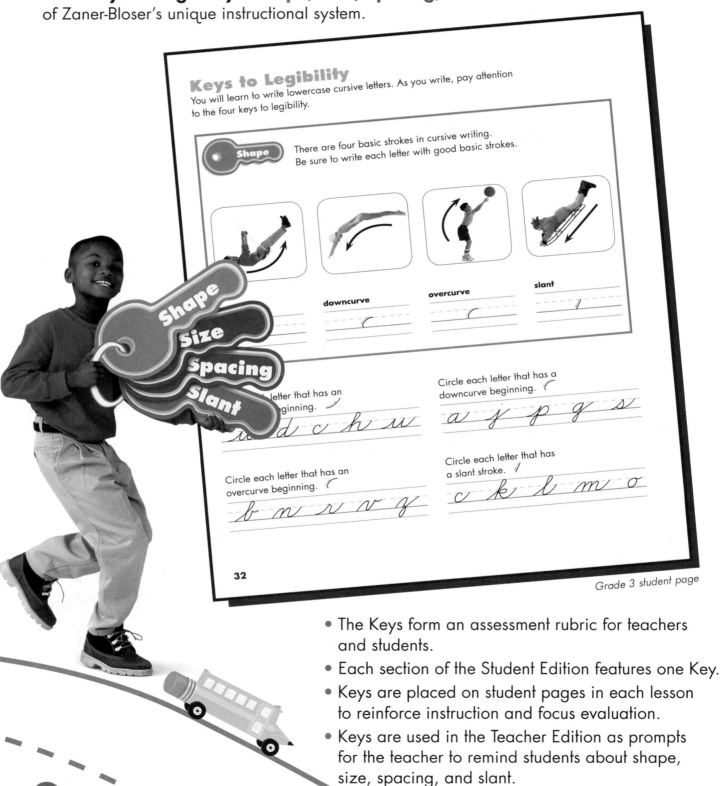

Keys to Legibility

You will learn to write lowercase cursive letters. As you write, pay attention to the four keys to legibility.

Shape — There are four basic strokes in cursive writing. Be sure to write each letter with good basic strokes.

downcurve

overcurve

slant

Circle each letter that has an [...] beginning.

_i d c h u_

Circle each letter that has a downcurve beginning.

_a j p q s_

Circle each letter that has an overcurve beginning.

_b n r v y_

Circle each letter that has a slant stroke.

_c k l m o_

32

Grade 3 student page

- The Keys form an assessment rubric for teachers and students.
- Each section of the Student Edition features one Key.
- Keys are placed on student pages in each lesson to reinforce instruction and focus evaluation.
- Keys are used in the Teacher Edition as prompts for the teacher to remind students about shape, size, spacing, and slant.

The Way to Better Assessment

Better Self-Assessment

 Stop and Check Signs throughout the lessons are reminders for students to continuously self-evaluate as they work.

 **Keys to Legibility** provide students with a system for learning and assessing their handwriting.

More Success on Standardized Tests

Writing Quickly provides a challenging exercise to help students develop automaticity in writing. This enables students to do well in high-pressure testing situations where they must write quickly and maintain legibility.

Writing Quickly

Writing quickly is a skill that will help when you need to write a story, take a timed test, or take notes.

Writing that is done quickly should still be easy to read. With practice, you will learn how to make your writing speedy and legible.

Read the saying. Write it quickly and legibly.

*In fourteen hundred
ninety-two Colum
sailed the ocean*

Now write the lines again.
Try to write them faster this time.

122

Write the saying two more times.
Try to write it even faster, but keep it easy to read.

Now read your final writing. Circle Yes or No to respond to each statement. Then show your writing to another reader, either a classmate or your teacher. Ask that person to circle Yes or No beside each statement.

	My Evaluation	My Classmate's or Teacher's Evaluation
The writing is easy to read.	Yes No	
The writing has good **Shape**.	Yes No	Yes No
The writing has good **Size**.	Yes No	Yes No
The writing has good **Spacing**.	Yes No	Yes No
The writing has good **Slant**.	Yes No	Yes No

123

Grade 3 student pages

What is automaticity?

The process in which individual letter formation occurs spontaneously and allows students to transfer their thoughts without interruption.

The Teacher Edition

Guide students down a proven path to legibility with flexible lesson plans that

- Can be part of any daily teaching routine
- Can be taught in as little as 15 minutes
- Work with any language arts curriculum to fully support reading and writing instruction
- Offer excellent cross-curricular opportunities

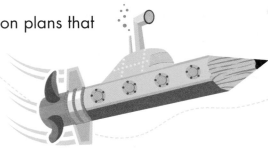

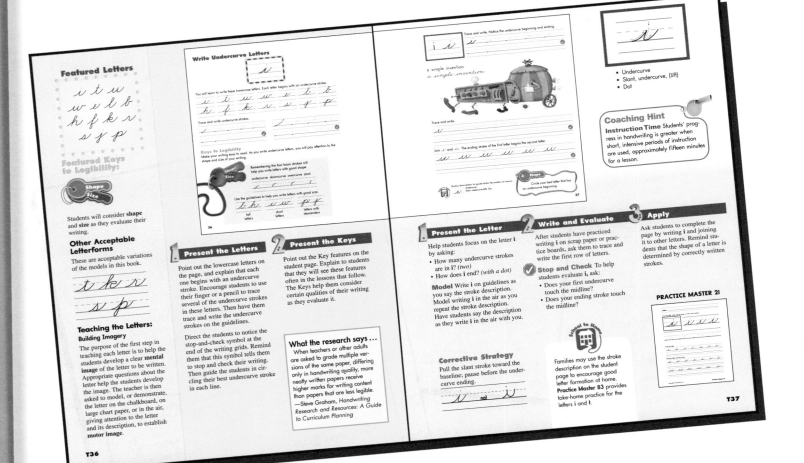

Grade 3 teacher edition pages

 **NEW** Every Teacher Edition contains **teacher tips, cultural notes,** and **additional resources** for teaching English-Language Learners.

3-Step Lesson

Takes 15 minutes!

The Three-Step Lesson presents a clear, simple instructional plan.

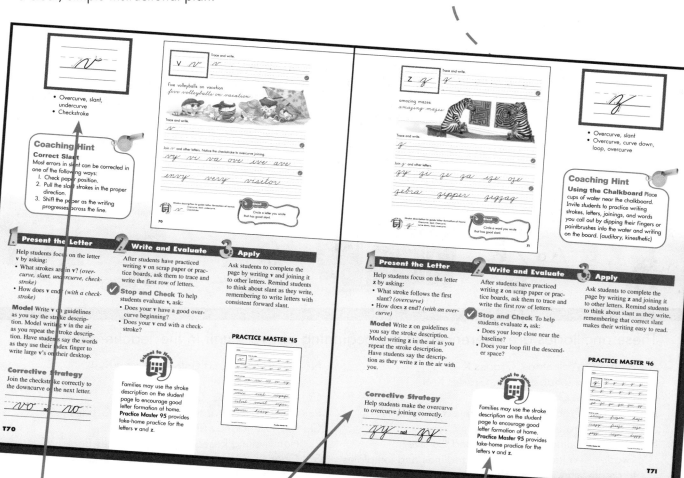

Grade 3 teacher edition pages

Stroke Descriptions are short and clear.

Corrective Strategies & Coaching Hints offer suggestions to correct common problems.

School-to-Home activities offer suggestions for involving families.

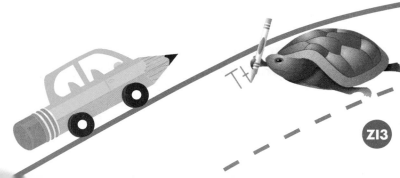

Ancillary Materials

These ancillaries are referenced at the beginning of every unit in the Teacher Edition.

A. Alphabet Wall Strips, Grades K–6
B. Illustrated Alphabet Strips, Grades K–4
C. Desk Strips, Grades 1–4
D. Wipe-Off Practice Cards—Manuscript and Cursive, Grades K–6
E. ZB Fonts Online—Manuscript and Cursive, Grades K–6 includes optional gridlines and templates to create work sheets, letters to parents, certificates and more! Found at www.zaner-bloser.com.
F. Manuscript/Cursive Card Sets, Grades 1–4
G Home Handwriting Pack, Grades K–4
H. Journals and Blank Books, Grades K–6
I. Paper, Grades K–6
J. Escritura—Spanish Blackline Masters, Grades 1–6
K. Touch and Trace Letter Cards—Manuscript and Cursive, PreK–Grade 3
L. Now I Know My ABCs, PreK–Grade 1
M. Now I Know My 1,2,3's, PreK–Grade 1

N. Read, Write, and Color Alphabet Mat, Grades K–2
O. Alphabet Cards, Grades K–2
P. Handwriting Transparency Books, Grades 1–6
Q. Fun With Handwriting
R. Handwriting Research and Resources Book
S. Opens the Door to Teaching Handwriting— Teacher Resource CD-ROM

Only Zaner-Bloser provides you with this much support for teaching handwriting!

Fine Motor Development Kit

Zaner-Bloser's Fine Motor Development Kit can help your students develop the fine-motor skills essential for writing and many other school activites.

Backed by Research

Research shows that handwriting is an important foundational skill. Research-supported **Zaner-Bloser Handwriting** is backed by decades of proven results, enabling teachers to give students the tools they need to be successful in reading, writing, and testing.

Reading

Zaner-Bloser Handwriting's vertical manuscript alphabet improves letter recognition and supports reading development.
"Solid familiarity with the visual shapes of the individual letters is an absolute prerequisite for learning to read."
—Marilyn Jager Adams, *Beginning to Read: Thinking and Learning About Print*

Writing

Zaner-Bloser Handwriting supports proficient writing skills.
In a study of first graders, researchers found that when children with poor handwriting received direct handwriting instruction, they improved in their writing, and the sample as a whole improved in word recognition, a skill that was not directly taught (Berninger, el al, 1997).

Standardized Testing

Zaner-Bloser Handwriting's systematic program builds automaticity and improves speed and legibility—all key factors in improving student's success on standardized tests.
"Students today are asked to write more, and write well. We expect them to master the writing process, and to demonstrate their proficiency on a variety of district and statewide tests. Faced with these high expectations for writing instruction, it is no suprise that educators have renewed interest in one of the most critical support skills for writing—handwriting."
—Steve Graham, *Handwriting Research and Resources: A Guide to Curriculum Planning*

The Way to Meet Individual Needs

English-Language Learners

Understanding Second Language Learning

Language learning is an involved and time-consuming process. Throughout this process, students will transition through several stages—moving from basic speech emergence to fluency.

Beginners/Emergent Learners Students at this level progress from a silent phase to the emergence of basic speech. At this beginning level, students may have 500 words in their receptive vocabulary. During the silent phase, they make use of observation and imitation. Through observation, students absorb what is going on in their immediate surroundings. They listen carefully to the language being used around them. They begin to imitate what others are doing and saying. Students are able to parrot what they hear, but may not understand the meaning of the words they are echoing. As students progress from the silent phase, they will begin to use one- and two-word phrases. Gradually, these phrases will evolve into simple sentences or questions.

To help students in this phase of language development:

- Focus on building students' receptive vocabulary.
- Ask students to answer yes-or-no questions.
- Have them copy words, participate in choral/echo reading, and respond to pictures and other visuals.
- Use Total Physical Response (TPR), a teaching approach that relies heavily on gestures and pantomime, to build vocabulary.
- Develop phonemic awareness through poetry and rhymes.

Intermediate Learners Students' vocabulary grows to approximately 6,000 active words. At this level, students begin using more complex sentences in both their oral and written communication. Because of their expanded vocabulary, students should be able to synthesize more complex concepts that are presented, and make inferences from what they have learned. Students are gaining confidence in their English-speaking ability and will be more willing to express opinions and share thoughts and ideas. Students often develop communicative fluency more readily at this stage than written accuracy and language correctness.

Intermediate Learners (continued)

To help students in this phase of language development:

- Continue developing students' understanding and use of vocabulary.
- Help students gain control of the English grammar system.
- Ask them questions with predictable responses.
- Have them make predictions, participate in discussions, describe past experiences, and summarize events.

Advanced/Fluent Learners It will take students five to ten years to reach this level of language acquisition. Students at this level perform at near-native fluency. They may still require some support, but should be able to function well within content-area learning.

Tips for Teachers of English-Language Learners

Build Phonemic Awareness

- Use visual cues to help students connect letters to beginning sounds. Always show the letter or letters that produce the sound you are teaching.
- Use poetry to introduce rhyming words and further develop phonemic awareness.

Build Vocabulary

- Label common classroom objects.
- Make extensive use of visuals. Always show an object as you say or write its name. Keep in mind that for ELL students, the written or spoken word may have little meaning.
- Use Total Physical Response to teach action words, commands, and content-specific vocabulary.
- Teach language necessary for social and academic contexts.
- Use visuals and repetition when giving directions. For example, when instructing students to open their books to a certain lesson, model the action that you want students to do and be consistent in your directive. Repeat the directive with the action consistently. For example, Open your books to page X, or, Turn to page X, but do not mix up your directives. This will confuse your students.
- Teach language along with content.

The Way to Meet Individual Needs

English-Language Learners (continued)

Build Literacy

- Read aloud to your students often. This models intonation and allows students to hear the sounds and structure of language.
- Encourage students to read aloud to family members in their first language. Reading skills necessary for comprehension are the same across cultures. If a student's reading comprehension skills are good in the student's dominant language, these skills will most likely transfer to a second language.
- Allow students to read a simplified or more accessible version of a text.
- Incorporate choral reading and echo reading into your instruction.

Build Writing Skills

- Use active voice.
- Model subject-verb-object sentence constructions.
- Scaffold writing instruction. Begin by providing students with the most support and gradually decrease your level of assistance until students become independent writers. (Early scaffolding may include cloze writing activities, stories that require students to fill in blanks, or filling in graphic organizers for students to use as part of a pre-writing activity.)

See the Appendix for Cultural Notes, School-to Home Issues, and a list of recommended Teacher Resources

Kinesthetic Learners

- Walk out the letter strokes on the floor.
- Form letters in the air using full-arm movement.
- Make letter models with clay or string.
- Use different writing instruments, such as crayons, markers, and varied sizes of pencils.
- Trace large strokes, letters, and joinings on the chalkboard and on paper—first with fingers, then with chalk or other media.

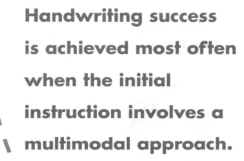

Auditory Learners

- Verbalize each stroke in the letter as that letter is presented.
- Encourage the student to verbalize the letter strokes and to explain how strokes are alike and how they are different in the letterforms.
- Ask students to write random letters as you verbalize the strokes.
- Be consistent in the language you use to describe letters, strokes, shapes, and joinings.

Handwriting success is achieved most often when the initial instruction involves a multimodal approach.

Visual Learners

- Encourage students first to look at the letter as a whole and to ask themselves if the letter is tall or short, fat or skinny. Does all of the letter rest on the baseline, is it a tall letter, or is it a letter with a descender? How many and what kinds of strokes are in the letter?
- Have students look at each individual stroke carefully before they attempt to write the letter.

The Way to Meet Individual Needs

Left-Handed Students

Three important techniques assist the left-handed student in writing.

**Manuscript
Paper Position**

Pencil Position

Paper Position

For manuscript writing, the lower right corner of the paper should point toward the left of the body's midsection. Downstrokes are pulled towards the left elbow.

For cursive writing, the lower right corner of the paper should point toward the body's midsection. Downstrokes are pulled toward the left elbow.

**Cursive
Paper Position**

Pencil Position

The top of the pencil should point toward the left elbow. The pen or pencil should be held at least one inch above the point. This allows students to see what they are writing.

Arm Position

Holding the left arm close to the body and keeping the hand below the line of writing prevents "hooking" the wrist and smearing the writing.

Students With ADD and ADHD

Because they have difficulty focusing and maintaining attention, ADD/ADHD students must concentrate on individual strokes in the letterforms. When they have learned the strokes, they can put them together to form letters, and then learn the joinings (in cursive) to write words. The activities recommended for kinesthetic learners (on page Z19) are appropriate for students with attention deficit problems. Following are additional suggestions:

- Give very short assignments.
- Supervise closely and give frequent encouragement.

Students With Reversal Tendencies

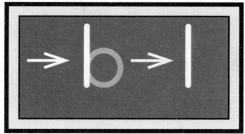 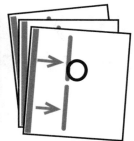

Directionality

A problem with directionality (moving from left to right across the page) interferes with a child's ability to form letters correctly and to write text that makes sense. To develop correct directionality, try these techniques:

- Provide opportunities for the child to write at the chalkboard within a confined area with frequent arrows as a reminder of left-to-right progression.
- Prepare sheets of paper on which the left edges and the beginning stroke of a letter, such as b, are colored green.

Letter Reversals

Determine which letters a student reverses most often. Make a list of these reversals and concentrate on them either on an individual basis or by grouping together the students who are reversing the same letters.

- Emphasize each step of the stroke description before the children write a letter.
- Provide a letter for tracing that has been colored according to stroke order. Repeat the stroke description with the children as they write the letter.
- Encourage the children to write the letter as they verbalize the stroke description.

The Way to Teach Handwriting in the 21st Century

An Occupational Therapist's Perspective

By Maureen King, O.T.R.

Developmental Skills

Children come to school with a broad range of developmental skill levels. Many children are already using many fine-motor skills, gross-motor skills, and perceptual skills, developed through exposure to a variety of play experiences. Some children, however, have not properly developed these fundamental skills that directly impact how well they learn in school.

Hand (motor) skills, as they develop, build upon each other, beginning at birth when babies grasp reflexively. As children grow and interact with their surroundings, they move on to using their thumbs and index fingers, and then their hands in a variety of positions. The development of perceptual skills, a child's ability to perceive how things fit together, is best facilitated by assembling and moving objects around.

Play and Handwriting

In the past, there were more "play-filled" opportunities to prompt development of these skills. Today, however, children's play is becoming more automated. Many board games are now played on computer screens, shoes are fastened with Velcro, and crayons are put aside in order to pursue interactive activities. This decreased use of manipulatives at home and at school can diminish a child's opportunity to practice grasp and release and controlled placement—skills that are necessary for efficient pencil use.

Symptoms of these trends can manifest themselves in a young child's first handwriting experiences at school. Handwriting requires eye-hand coordination fine-motor skills, and the perceptual ability to simultaneously understand and produce letterforms. When children who have not developed key foundational skills first attempt to write manuscript letters, frustration can result. Often, their efforts consist of incomplete or careless methods of forming letters, which can lead to bad habits. Something must be done for these children so that they can achieve handwriting success.

Corrective Strategies

I am pleased to offer structured corrective strategies that will help teachers strengthen skills that lead to improved handwriting. You will find these strategies, or Special Helps, throughout the Zaner-Bloser Handwriting Teacher Edition. They suggest ways to isolate component skills, reinforce the instructional material, and highlight special points and concerns. In using these ideas in your classroom, include a mix of learning styles so that children can see it, hear it, feel it, do it in their palms and on the chalkboard, with their eyes open and closed. These activities will help bring handwriting success to all children, including those who rarely play board games, color with crayons, or tie their shoes.

Maureen King provides Special Help tips throughout the Grade K–3 Teacher Editions.

The Way to Introduce Handwriting to Young Children

Zaner-Bloser has created a developmentally-appropriate program to introduce children to written communication. **On the Road to Writing and Reading** uses songs, stories, movement, and manipulatives to create activities that complement any PreKindergarten curriculum.

Kit includes:

- Teacher Guide
- "Music, Mazes & More" CD-ROM (included in Teacher Guide)
- Group Time Cards
- Alphabet Cards
- Take-Home Posters (English and Spanish)
- Wikki Stix®
- Touch and Trace Manuscript Letter Cards
- Magnetic Board and Letters
- Blank Story Journal

Music, Mazes & More CD-ROM

Group Time Cards

Touch and Trace Manuscript Letter Cards

Take-Home Posters

Alphabet Cards

Magnetic Board and Letters

Wikki Stix®

Blank Story Journal

Z23

Zaner-Bloser Handwriting Workshops

Discover proven techniques for teaching manuscript and cursive handwriting!

- Learn fun activities to improve students' handwriting and standardized test scores
- Enhance your current handwriting instruction with developmentally-appropriate techniques
- Effectively implement a handwriting program that takes only 15 minutes a day
- Receive free classroom materials

 For locations and a detailed workshop agenda, call 800.505.5536, or visit www.zaner-bloser.com

Zaner-Bloser National Handwriting Contest

Over 140,000 participants each year!

- Open to all students in grades 1–8
- Prizes for students, teachers, and schools
- Great for assemblies—schools can award grade-level winners
- Can be completed in class, or at home
- Every student earns a participation certificate
- Free and Fun!

Enter TODAY!

 For more information, call 800.924.9233, or visit www.zaner-bloser.com

3

Zaner-Bloser
Handwriting

3

Author
Clinton S. Hackney, Ed.D.

Reviewers

Julie Althide, Teacher, Hazelwood School District, St. Louis, Missouri

Becky Brashears, Teacher, Gocio Elementary, Sarasota, Florida

Douglas Dewey, Teacher, National Heritage Academies, Grand Rapids, Michigan

Jennifer B. Dutcher, Teacher, Elk Grove School District, Sacramento, California

Gita Farbman, Teacher, School District of Philadelphia, Philadelphia, Pennsylvania

Susan Ford, Teacher, St. Ann's School, Charlotte, North Carolina

Brenda Forehand, Teacher, David Lipscomb Middle School, Nashville, Tennessee

Sharon Hall, Teacher, USD 443, Dodge City, Kansas

Sr. James Madeline, Teacher, St. Anthony School, Allston, Massachusetts

Lori A. Martin, Teacher, Chicago Public Schools, Chicago, Illinois

Vikki F. McCurdy, Teacher, Mustang School District, Oklahoma City, Oklahoma

Melissa Neary Morgan, Reading Specialist, Fairfax County Public Schools, Fairfax, Virginia

Sue Postlewait, Literacy Resource Consultant, Marshall County Schools, Moundsville, West Virginia

Gloria C. Rivera, Principal, Edinburg CISO, Edinburg, Texas

Rebecca Rollefson, Teacher, Ericsson Community School, Minneapolis, Minnesota

Susan Samsa, Teacher, Dover City Schools, Dover, Ohio

Zelda J. Smith, Instructional Specialist, New Orleans Public Schools, New Orleans, Louisiana

Occupational Therapy Consultant: Maureen E. King, O.T.R.

Credits

Art: Diane Blasius: 66, 67, 68, 69, 70, 71, 72, 73, 103, 104, 105, 106, 107, 108, 109; Liz Callen: 3, 18, 19, 25, 54, 55, 56, 57, 58, 59, 60, 61, 89, 90, 91, 92, 93, 94, 95, 96, 97, 98, 99, 100, 101, 121, 124; Keith Graves: 3, 4, 37, 38, 39, 40, 41, 42, 43, 44, 45, 46, 47, 48, 49, 50, 51, 52, 111, 112, 113, 114, 115, 116, 117, 118; John Hovell: 3, 33, 34, 35, 36, 53, 65, 78, 79, 80, 88, 102, 110, 126; Tom Leonard: 3, 64, 122; Susan Lexa: 8, 9, 10, 11, 12, 13, 14, 15, 16, 17, 20, 21, 22, 23, 62, 63, 76, 120; Troy Viss: 81, 82, 83, 84, 85, 86, 87

Photos: George C. Anderson Photography, Inc.: 5, 6, 26, 27; Stephen Ogilvy: 28, 29, 30, 31, 32, 78

Development: Kirchoff/Wohlberg, Inc., in collaboration with Zaner-Bloser Educational Publishers

ISBN-13 978-0-7367-5146-9   07 08 09 10 11   4495   5 4 3 2 1
ISBN-10 0-7367-5146-7

Copyright © 2008 Zaner-Bloser, Inc.

Zaner-Bloser, Inc., P.O. Box 16764, Columbus, Ohio 43216-6764
1-800-421-3018
www.zaner-bloser.com
Printed in the United States of America

Contents

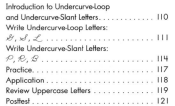

Legibility Is Important

The goal of *Zaner-Bloser Handwriting* is to teach students to write legibly. As you work through the pages of this book with the students, you will be helping them learn to write letters, words, and sentences that are legible to both writers and readers. By learning and applying the four Keys to Legibility—**shape, size, spacing,** and **slant**—the students will evaluate their writing and discover techniques to help them improve and refine their writing skills.

The opening pages are important for laying a foundation for writing. An **Optional Manuscript Review** helps the students warm up for cursive writing. A **Pretest** provides an initial sample of the students' handwriting quality before the year's formal handwriting instruction. **Welcome to Cursive** provides readiness information for beginning cursive writing. **Cursive Letters and Numerals** presents correct models of the forms the students will write. **Writing Positions** guides students in the correct positions for sitting, holding the writing implement, and positioning the paper. On the pages for **Basic Strokes,** students will become familiar with the lines that form all the letters and numerals in cursive handwriting. The **Keys to Legibility** describe the qualities of good writing that will help students evaluate and improve their writing throughout the year.

Lowercase and uppercase letters are introduced separately. The letter sequence is determined by the beginning stroke of the letters. In **Writing Numerals,** students observe models and write the cursive numerals **1** through **10** with correct strokes. Finally, students are encouraged to increase their speed and fluency as they gain automaticity in handwriting.

Note that models are provided for all writing, and students have space to write directly beneath the models. A **Key** feature on every letter page fosters self-evaluation on a continuing basis.

It is suggested that students keep a writing notebook or folder of the writing they do for themselves and for others.

Use this introductory page with your class as an invitation to the *Zaner-Bloser Handwriting* program. It defines and explains the visual components on the student page that help them learn to write and evaluate with consistency.

Explain to students that in this book they will learn how to write letters, words, and sentences. They will also discover ways to help make their writing easy to read.

Practice Masters

- Review of Manuscript Writing, 1–8
- Cursive Readiness, 9–20
- Letters, 21–72
- Numerals, 73–74
- Record of Student's Handwriting Skills, 75
- Certificates, 76–77
- Manuscript Alphabet, 78
- Cursive Alphabet, 79
- Cursive Stroke Descriptions, 80–82
- School-to-Home Practice Pages, 83–108
- Blank Writing Grid, 109

These support products are available in Zaner-Bloser's K–8 Catalog.

- Poster/Wall Chart Super Pack
- Touch and Trace Letter Cards
- Alphabet Wall Strips
- Wipe-Off Practice Cards
- Zaner-Bloser Fontware
- Manuscript/Cursive Card Sets
- Home Handwriting Pack
- Evaluation Guide
- Handwriting Helper Kit
- Journals and Blank Books
- Transparencies
- *Opens the Door to Teaching Handwriting* (CD-ROM)
- *Handwriting Research and Resources*
- *Fun With Handwriting*
- *Escritura*

Grammar

Verbs, p. T16 Explain that the words listed on student page 16 are action verbs—words that name an action. Say each verb and pantomime the action it names. Then say each verb again and have students pantomime the action.

Beginner/Emergent Speakers: Create a verb dictionary. Tell students to choose a verb from the list and draw a picture to illustrate the action it names. Students should write the selected verb at the bottom of the illustration. Collect students' illustrations, have a student alphabetize the entries, then bind them.

Intermediate Speakers: Write action verbs on strips of paper and place the strips into an empty box or container. Invite a volunteer to select a verb from the box and pantomime its action. The first student to name the verb correctly gets to choose the next one to pantomime.

Advanced/Fluent Speakers: Help students apply the use of verbs in their writing. Make a two-column chart on the board. Label the first column "Who" and the second column "Did What." Write simple sentences on the board, using the names of your students as subjects and the verbs from the list on student page 16 as predicates. Invite a different volunteer to read each sentence. Ask students: "Who is [doing the action]? What is [student's name] doing?" Write student responses in the correct column on the board. After students have practiced all the verbs on the list, challenge them to create original sentences.

Vocabulary Development

Homophones, p. T16 Explain that some English words are pronounced the same way but have different meanings and may have different spellings. Use the words *March* and *march* as examples. Create word cards with illustrations that show the meaning of each word. As you share each card, use describing words and phrases, and gestures and pantomime as appropriate, to help explain the meanings. For example, "March is the third month of the year. When we march, we step in rhythm." Demonstrate marching.

Beginner/Emergent Speakers: Pose riddles or questions for which the answer is one of the words in the homophone pair. Say, "I am the third month of the year" or "I come after February." Have students point to the card that indicates the correct answer.

Intermediate Speakers: Create a cloze activity in which students complete sentences by inserting either *March* or *march*.

Advanced/Fluent Speakers: Have partners take turns making up riddles or asking questions to which the answer is one of the words in the homophone pair.

Basic Strokes, pp. T8–T15 Show students what it means to *pull down straight*. Invite students to stand with you, arms stretched up toward the ceiling. Make a motion as though you are pulling down. Have students mimic your actions. Then show students what it means to *slide right*. Move in a sliding motion to the right as you say "slide right." Have students mimic your actions. Next, ask students to be seated and to take out a pencil and paper. Instruct them to position pencils on the headline and pull down straight. Explain that doing so forms a vertical line. Have students practice making vertical lines. Then, instruct students to place their pencils on the headline and slide right. Explain that doing so forms a horizontal line. Have students practice making horizontal lines.

Specific Teaching Tips

Developing listening skills is an important part of language acquisition. Use commands and Total Physical Response (TPR) to help students develop listening skills. Your students' physical responses to your commands will add to their understanding of the language and demonstrate comprehension of your words.

Coaching Hint

Using the Chalkboard, p. T6 As you present material orally, or write on the board, remember that students make use of both verbal and non-verbal cues. When writing on the board, position yourself so that students can see you when you are speaking. Doing so allows students to watch your facial expressions and look for other non-verbal cues, listen to your intonation without the sound being muffled, and observe how you are producing the sounds you are speaking.

Coaching Hint

Manuscript Writing, p. T7 Provide students with opportunities to practice using content and functional vocabulary in meaningful ways. Make learning more meaningful when you link content to students' experiences and background. For example, ask students to compare what they have observed on a field trip to situations or events familiar to them.

Beginner/Emergent Speakers: Have students complete writing activities that focus on basic skills, such as letter formation (both manuscript and cursive); spelling patterns; rules of capitalization and punctuation; and word and sentence order. Appropriate activities include labeling, making lists, and alphabetizing.

Intermediate and Advanced/Fluent Speakers: As students' knowledge of English increases, they can begin extended writing tasks. Students should engage in guided composition, structuring sentences and paragraphs and questions and answers. Appropriate activities include writing about field trips, retelling a story, and writing original stories, poems, and descriptions.

Coaching Hint

Practice, p. T17 Use these activities to improve letter and word recognition skills, build vocabulary, and reinforce English writing conventions.

Label pictures and objects. Students can use the labeled pictures to create picture dictionaries.

Solve word-search puzzles. Students can practice letter and word recognition.

List items by category. Use listed words to build vocabulary. For example, after students write a list of lunch foods, use those words as you model how to express personal preferences. Introduce these words and phrases: *like, my favorite,* and *don't like.* Then say or write: "I like pretzels. I don't like salt and vinegar potato chips. Tacos are my favorite food."

Practice writing conventions. Engaging students in writing stories, poems, and descriptions, retelling stories, and listing facts will expose them to the four basic sentence types. Help students understand the most basic English writing convention: Sentences start with a capital letter and end with some form of punctuation. When giving students practice sentences, point out that the first letter of each sentence is capitalized. Then draw students' attention to the end of the sentence. Explain that punctuation tells readers when to pause and when a thought ends. Stress the importance of including punctuation at the end of every sentence. Explain when and how to use each form of punctuation.

Retell stories. Students practice English and demonstrate comprehension by retelling stories. Encourage students with only rudimentary proficiency in English to use pictures, puppets, or dramatization in their retelling.

CULTURAL NOTES

The English writing system uses a left-to-right, top-to-bottom directional system. Some language systems, such as in the Middle East, use a right-to-left, top-to-bottom direction. Certain Asian languages use top-to-bottom, right-to-left direction. Remind students to use the proper directionality when writing.

Manuscript Review

Writing Positions: Manuscript

Suggest that students refer to this page throughout the year as a reminder of correct paper and pencil position for manuscript writing. Demonstrate correct positions for both left-handed and right-handed writers. Then ask students to place a sheet of paper in the proper position on their desks, pick up a pencil, and write their names.

Coaching Hint

Using the Chalkboard
You and your students can follow these suggestions for writing on the chalkboard.

Left-Handed Writers Stand in front of the writing lines and pull the downstrokes to the left elbow. The elbow is bent, and the writing is done at a comfortable height. Step to the right often to maintain correct slant.

Right-Handed Writers Stand to the left of the writing lines and pull the downstrokes toward the midsection of the body. The elbow is bent, and the writing is done at a comfortable height. Step to the right often to maintain correct slant. (visual, kinesthetic)

Alternate Pencil Position

Students who have difficulty with the traditional pencil position may prefer the alternate method of holding the pencil between the first and second fingers.

Manuscript Review

Reviewing Manuscript Writing

People use manuscript writing every day. Good manuscript writing is easy to read.

Be sure to put your paper in the correct position for manuscript when you write. That will help keep your writing straight up and down.

Writing Positions: Manuscript

If you write with your left hand. . .   If you write with your right hand. . .

Place the paper like this.   **Place the paper like this.**

Slant the paper as shown in the picture.   Place the paper straight in front of you.

Rest both arms on the desk. Use your right hand to move the paper as you write.   Rest both arms on the desk. Use your left hand to move the paper as you write.

Pull the pencil toward your left elbow when you write.   Pull the pencil toward the middle of your body when you write.

Hold the pencil like this.   **Hold the pencil like this.**

Hold the pencil with your thumb and first two fingers. Do not squeeze the pencil when you write.

6

Paper Position Correct page placement is a critical factor in legibility. To ensure that the paper is placed correctly for both right- and left-handed students, use tape to form a frame on the desk so the students will be able to place the paper in the correct position.

left-handed writers   **right-handed writers**

Pencil Position Model good pencil position for the students. The writing implement is held between the thumb and the first two fingers, about an inch above its point. The first finger rests on the top of the implement. The end of the bent thumb is placed against the writing instrument to hold it high in the hand and near the knuckle.

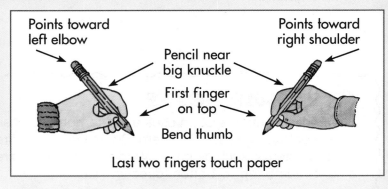

Points toward left elbow   Points toward right shoulder

Pencil near big knuckle

First finger on top

Bend thumb

Last two fingers touch paper

Keys to Legibility

Make your writing easy to read.

Shape

Look at the shape of these letters.
Trace the letters.

Manuscript letters contain vertical lines (|),
horizontal lines (—), circle lines (O ( )), and
slant lines (\ /).

✔ Circle each type of line in the
letters above.

Size

Look at the size of these letters.
Trace the letters.

Tall letters touch the headline. Short letters
touch the midline. Letters with descenders go
below the baseline and touch the next line.

✔ Circle a short letter. Underline a tall
letter. Draw a box around a letter with
a descender.

Spacing

Look at the spacing of this writing.
Trace the words.

The letters are not too close together
or too far apart.

There is enough space for a paper clip
between words.

✔ Use a paper clip or your little
finger to measure the spacing
between the words above.

Slant

Look at the vertical slant of this writing.
Trace the word.

Manuscript letters are straight up and down.
To write with good slant:

1. Place your paper correctly.
2. Pull down in the proper direction.
3. Shift your paper as you write.

✔ Draw lines through the vertical strokes in
the letters above. If your lines are straight,
then the writing has good slant.

7

Keys to Legibility

Point out the key logos on student page 7. Explain to students that they will see these key symbols often. Each key directs the students to consider certain qualities of good writing as they evaluate their work.

Shape The basic strokes—vertical, horizontal, circle, slant—written correctly in specific combinations yield letters with correct shape.

Size Forming letters that are correctly placed on guidelines yields letters with correct size.

Spacing Letters and words that are too close together or too far apart are hard to read.

Slant In manuscript writing, letters are written with vertical slant. The correct position of the paper and the proper direction in which the strokes are pulled foster vertical slant.

Review the Keys

Direct the students to notice the four separate sections on student page 7. Point out that each section reviews a specific Key to Legibility for manuscript writing. Emphasize to students that applying the keys consistently as they write will promote the legibility of their writing.

With the students, work through the information provided for each key. Use the chalkboard as needed to model and reinforce what the students are reviewing.

Coaching Hints

At the Chalkboard Use manuscript writing on the chalkboard for various purposes, especially vocabulary and dictionary study, as well as other work involving word attack skills. (visual, kinesthetic)

Manuscript Writing Give a weekly assignment that requires students to use their best manuscript writing, such as filling out forms, doing map study, developing charts, preparing labels and captions, working crossword puzzles, and making posters. (visual, kinesthetic)

See the **Keys to Legibility Wall Chart** *for more information.*

Pull down straight.

 Pull down straight.
Slide right.

 Pull down straight.
Lift. Dot.

 Pull down straight.
Lift. Slide right.
Lift. Slide right.

 Pull down straight.
Lift. Slide right.

Pull down straight.
Lift. Slide right.

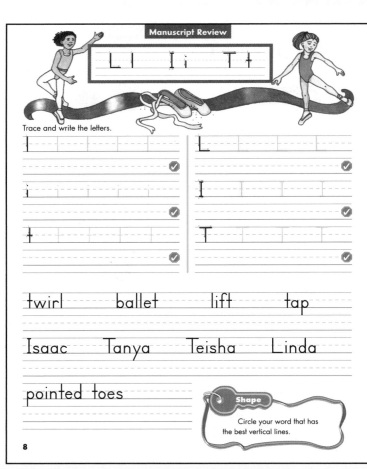

L l   I i   T t

Trace and write the letters.

l   L

i   I

t   T

twirl   ballet   lift   tap

Isaac   Tanya   Teisha   Linda

pointed toes

Shape
Circle your word that has
the best vertical lines.

8

1 Present the Letters

Direct students to look at the letter models. To help students focus on the letters, ask:

- Which stroke begins each letter?
- Which letter is short?
- Which letters are tall?
- Which letters have slide right strokes?

Model Write the letters on guidelines as you say the stroke descriptions. Repeat the stroke descriptions as the students use their finger to trace the letters on their desktop.

Corrective Strategy

The pull down straight stroke should be pulled, not drawn.

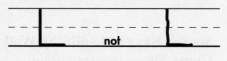

not

2 Write and Evaluate

After students have practiced writing the letters on marker boards or slates or on other paper, ask them to trace and write each letter on the page. Remind students to take time to write each letter carefully.

 Stop and Check This icon directs students to stop and circle their best letter.

To help students evaluate, ask:

- Is your **l** straight up and down?
- Does your **L** begin at the headline?
- Did you to dot your **i**?
- Is your **I** about the same width as the model?
- Is the vertical line in your **t** straight?
- Is the slide right stroke in **T** written on the headline?

3 Apply

Before students write words to complete the page, call attention to the shape of the letters. Ask volunteers to point out letters that are written with vertical, horizontal, circle, and slant lines. After students write, guide them in completing the direction in the Key feature at the bottom of the page.

PRACTICE MASTER 1

Manuscript Review
Write the letters.

Write the words.
label   lullaby   icicle
inside   twist   tablet
Leslie   Lancelot   Iris
Iberia   Tahiti   Trevor

Copyright © Zaner-Bloser, Inc.   Practice Master 1

T8

Manuscript Review

O o A a D d

Trace and write the letters.

o o o o o
a a a a a
d d d d d

O O O O
A A A A
D D D D

Write the words.

glove   hooray   double   baseball

Donald   Todd   Anna   Olaf

second base

Size
Circle your best tall letter.

9

Circle back all the way around.

Circle back all the way around.

Circle back all the way around; push up straight. Pull down straight.

Slant left. Lift. Slant right. Lift. Slide right.

Circle back all the way around; push up straight. Pull down straight.

Pull down straight. Lift. Slide right; curve forward; slide left.

---

1. Present the Letters

Direct students to look at the letter models. To help students focus on the letters, ask:

- Which letters are tall?
- Which letters have a circle back stroke?
- Which letters look alike except for their size?

Model Write the letters on guidelines as you say the stroke descriptions. Have students use their finger to trace the models in their books as you repeat the descriptions.

Corrective Strategy

The circle back stroke should form a complete, round circle.

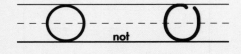
not

2. Write and Evaluate

After students have practiced writing the letters on marker boards or slates or on other paper, ask them to trace and write each letter on the page. Remind students to take time to write each letter carefully.

Stop and Check To help students evaluate, ask:

- Does your **o** begin just below the midline?
- Are your **o** and **O** round?
- Does your vertical stroke in **a** touch the circle?
- Is your **A** about the same width as the model?
- Is the backward circle in your **d** round?
- Is the curve forward stroke in your **D** rounded?

3. Apply

Before students write words to complete the page, call attention to the size of the letters. Ask them to point out tall letters, short letters, and short letters with descenders. After students write, guide them in completing the direction in the Key feature at the bottom of the page.

PRACTICE MASTER 2

Manuscript Review

Write the letters.

o o o o   O O O O
a a a a   A A A A
d d d d   D D D D

Write the words.

wool   odd   aloha
agenda   demand   dazed
Oslo   Oscar   Andrea
Asia   Dirk   Denise

Practice Master 2   Copyright © Zaner-Bloser, Inc.

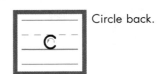 Circle back.

 Circle back.

 Slide right.
Circle back.

 Pull down straight.
Lift. Slide right.
Lift. Slide right;
stop short. Lift.
Slide right.

 Curve back; pull
down straight. Lift.
Slide right.

 Pull down straight.
Lift. Slide right.
Lift. Slide right;
stop short.

Manuscript Review

C c   E e   F f

Now Showing   The Lion and the Mouse

Trace and write the letters.

c c c c c c   C C C C

e e e e e e   E E

f f f f f f   F F

Write the words.

stage   fierce   cute   clap

Cliff   Effie   Fran   Ella

fun costumes

Spacing
Circle two letters with good spacing between them.

10

---

 1 Present the Letters

Direct students to look at the letter models. To help students focus on the letters, ask:

- Which letters have a vertical stroke?
- Which letter has two slide right strokes?
- Which letters have a circle back stroke?

Model Write the letters on guidelines as you say the stroke descriptions. Have students say them as they write the letters in the air with you.

Corrective Strategy

The circle back stroke must touch the slide right stroke.

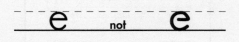

e not e

TIO

2 Write and Evaluate

After students have practiced writing the letters on marker boards or slates or on other paper, ask them to trace and write each letter on the page. Remind students to take time to write each letter carefully.

✓ **Stop and Check** To help students evaluate, ask:

- Is your **c** written between the midline and the baseline?
- Does your **C** look like a circle that has not been closed?
- Does your slide right stroke in **e** touch your circle back stroke?
- Are the top and bottom slide right strokes in your **E** the same width?
- Does your **f** begin below the headline?
- Is your vertical line in **F** straight?

3 Apply

Before students write words to complete the page, ask them to pay attention to the spacing between letters. In legible writing, letters should not be so close together or so far apart that confusion occurs. After students write, guide them in completing the direction in the Key feature at the bottom of the page.

PRACTICE MASTER 3

Manuscript Review

Write the letters.
c c c c   C C C C
e e e e   E E E E
f f f f   F F F F

Write the words.
cactus   crutch   engine
evening   cliff   fifty
Canada   Carson   Enid
Elvis   France   Faith

Copyright © Zaner-Bloser, Inc.   Practice Master 3

G g   J j   Q q

Trace and write the letters.

g g g g g ✓   G G G G ✓

j j j j j ✓   J J J J ✓

q q q q q ✓   Q Q Q Q ✓

Write the words.

juggle   equipment   enjoy   quit

Jay   Ginny   Juan   Quito

quick juggler

Slant

Circle your word that has the best vertical slant.

II

Circle back all the way around; push up straight. Pull down straight; curve back.

Circle back. Slide left.

Pull down straight; curve back. Lift. Dot.

Pull down straight; curve back. Lift. Slide right.

Circle back all the way around; push up straight. Pull down straight; curve forward.

Circle back all the way around. Lift. Slant right.

---

1 Present the Letters

Direct students to look at the letter models. To help the students focus on the letters, ask:

- Which letters begin with a vertical stroke?
- Which letters have a circle back stroke?
- Which letter has a descender that curves forward?

Model Write the letters on guidelines on the chalkboard as you say the stroke descriptions. Repeat the stroke descriptions as the students use their finger to write the letters on their desktop.

Corrective Strategy

The descender should touch the next headline.

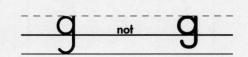

g   not   g

2 Write and Evaluate

After students have practiced writing the letters on marker boards or slates or on other paper, ask them to trace and write each letter on the page. Remind students to take time to write each letter carefully.

✓ **Stop and Check** To help students evaluate, ask:

- Is the circle back stroke of your **g** round?
- Is your **G** about the same width as the model?
- Did you dot your **j**?
- Is your **J** straight up and down?
- Does the descender line of your **q** touch the next headline?
- Does your **Q** look like an **O** except for the slant right stroke?

3 Apply

Before students write words to complete the page, call attention to the slant of the letters. Remind students that manuscript letters are vertical, or straight up and down. After students write, guide them in completing the direction in the Key feature at the bottom of the page.

PRACTICE MASTER 4

Manuscript Review

Write the letters.

g g g g   G G G G

j j j j   J J J J

q q q q   Q Q Q Q

Write the words.

garage   engineer   eject

jade   square   quiz

Greece   Gus   June

Jesse   Quincy   Qatar

Practice Master 4   Copyright © Zaner-Bloser, Inc.

Pull down straight; curve forward; push up. Pull down straight.

Pull down straight; curve forward; push up.

Curve back; curve forward.

Curve back; curve forward.

Pull down straight; push up. Circle forward.

Pull down straight. Lift. Slide right; curve forward; slide left. Slide right; curve forward; slide left.

Pull down straight. Push up. Circle forward all the way around.

Pull down straight. Lift. Slide right; curve forward; slide left.

U u S s B b P p

Trace and write the letters.

u u u u u   U U U U
s s s s s   S S S S
b b b b b   B B B B
p p p p p   P P P P

Write the words.

paint   use   splatter   brush   Bess

Paul   Samuel

Shape

Circle your best letter that has a circle line.

12

Present the Letters

Direct students to look at the letter models. To help students focus on the letters, ask:
- Which stroke begins **u** and **U**?
- How are **s** and **S** different?
- Which letters are tall?
- Which letter has a long retrace?

Model Write the letters on guidelines as you say the stroke descriptions. Repeat the stroke descriptions as the students use their finger to write the letters on their desktop.

Corrective Strategy

The slide right and slide left strokes are equal in width.

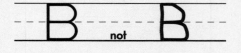

Write and Evaluate

After students have practiced writing the letters on marker boards or slates or on other paper, ask them to trace and write each letter.

✓ **Stop and Check** To help students evaluate, ask:
- Are the pull down straight strokes in your **u** straight?
- Does the curve of your **U** begin and end about halfway between the midline and baseline?
- Does your **s** begin just below the midline?
- Is the top of your **S** about the same size as the bottom?
- Is the vertical line in your **b** straight?
- Is your **B** about the same width as the model?
- Does your **p** begin at the midline?
- Is the slide left in your **P** on the midline?

Apply

Before students write words to complete the page, ask students to look at the page and point out strokes they recognize in the letters. Point out that correctly written strokes make correctly formed letters. After students write, guide them in completing the direction in the Key feature at the bottom of the page.

PRACTICE MASTER 5

Manuscript Review

Write the letters.

u u u u   U U U U
s s s s   S S S S
b b b b   B B B B
p p p p   P P P P

Write the words.

umbrella   sunset   bubble
pulp   Ulster   Solon
Savannah   Bernice   Peru

Copyright © Zaner-Bloser, Inc.   Practice Master 5

T12

R r   N n   M m   H h

Trace and write the letters.

r
n
m
h

R
N
M
H

Write the words.

musician   song   Nan   Hannah

Mark   Ron

Size
Circle your best short letter.

13

Pull down straight. Push up; curve forward.

Pull down straight. Lift. Slide right; curve forward; slide left. Slant right.

Pull down straight. Push up; curve forward; pull down straight.

Pull down straight. Lift. Slant right. Push up straight.

Pull down straight. Push up; curve forward; pull down straight. Push up; curve forward; pull down straight.

Pull down straight. Lift. Slant right. Slant up. Pull down straight.

Pull down straight. Push up; curve forward; pull down straight.

Pull down straight. Lift. Pull down straight. Lift. Slide right.

---

1. Present the Letters

Direct students to look at the letter models. Help them compare the letters by asking:

- Which stroke begins **r** and **R**?
- Which letters have a curve forward stroke?
- Which stroke begins **n** and **N**?
- How are **M** and **H** alike?

Model Write the letters on guidelines on the chalkboard as you say the stroke descriptions. Have students use their finger to trace the models in their book as you repeat the descriptions.

Corrective Strategy

Retrace carefully to avoid making a loop.

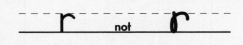
r   not   r

2. Write and Evaluate

After students have practiced writing the letters on marker boards or slates or on other paper, ask them to trace and write each letter on the page.

✓ **Stop and Check** To help students evaluate, ask:

- Did you retrace carefully in your **r**?
- Is your **R** vertical?
- Are the pull down straight strokes in your **n** straight?
- Is your **N** about the same width as the model?
- Are the vertical lines in your **m** straight?
- Does your **M** touch both the headline and the baseline?
- Does your **h** begin at the headline?
- Is the slide right in your **H** on the midline?

3. Apply

Before students write words to complete the page, review the three guidelines—headline, midline, and baseline. Point out that the guidelines help students write letters with correct size. After students write, guide them in completing the direction in the Key feature at the bottom of the page.

PRACTICE MASTER 6

Manuscript Review

Write the letters.

r   r   r   r   R R R R
n   n   n   n   N N N N
m   m   m   m   M M M M
h   h   h   h   H H H H

Write the words.

murmur   nation   memory
hatch   Ross   Netherlands
Mexico   Mike   Holly

Practice Master 6   Copyright © Zaner-Bloser, Inc.

T13

Slant right.
Slant up.

 Slant right. Lift.
Slant left.

 Slant right.
Slant up.
Slant right.
Slant up.

 Slant right.
Slant up.

 Slant right. Lift.
Slant left. Pull
down straight.

 Slant right.
Slant up.
Slant right.
Slant up.

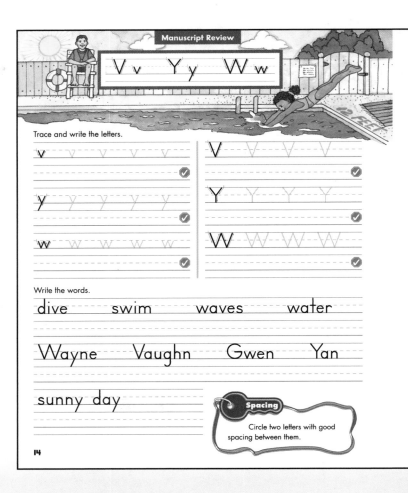

1. Present the Letters

Direct students to look at the letter models. To help students focus on the letters, ask:

- Which stroke begins each letter?
- How are **w** and **W** different?
- Which letter has a descender that goes below the baseline?

Model Write the letters on guidelines as you say the stroke descriptions. Repeat the stroke descriptions as the students use their finger to trace the letters on their desktop.

Corrective Strategy

The letter **Y** ends with a pull down straight stroke.

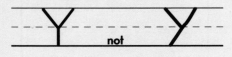

2. Write and Evaluate

After students have practiced writing the letters on marker boards or slates or on other paper, ask them to trace and write each letter. Remind students to take time to write each letter carefully.

Stop and Check To help students evaluate, ask:

- Are your slant strokes in **v** straight?
- Is your **V** about the same width as the model?
- Does your **y** touch the next headline?
- Does your **Y** end with a vertical stroke?
- Are the slant strokes in your **w** straight?
- Does your **W** begin at the headline?

3. Apply

Before students write words to complete the page, call attention to the spacing between the words *sunny* and *day*. Point out that there should be enough space for a small paper clip between words. After students write, guide them in completing the direction in the Key feature at the bottom of the page.

PRACTICE MASTER 7

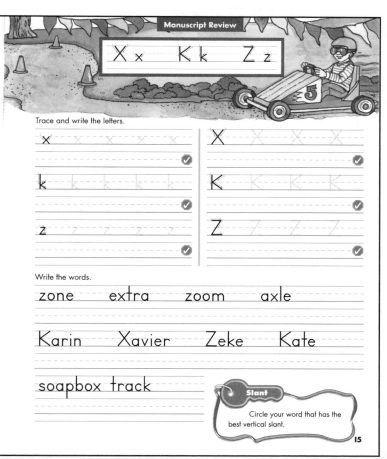

Manuscript Review

X x   K k   Z z

Trace and write the letters.

x x x x x x x
X X X X X
k k k k k k
K K K K K
z z z z z z z
Z Z Z Z Z

Write the words.

zone   extra   zoom   axle

Karin   Xavier   Zeke   Kate

soapbox track

Slant
Circle your word that has the best vertical slant.

15

Slant right. Lift. Slant left.

Slant right. Lift. Slant left.

Pull down straight. Lift. Slant left. Slant right.

Pull down straight. Lift. Slant left. Slant right.

Slide right. Slant left. Slide right.

Slide right. Slant left. Slide right.

1 Present the Letters

Direct students to look at the letter models. Help them compare the letters by asking:

- Which stroke begins **x** and **X**?
- Which letters have a pull down straight stroke?
- Which letters have slant strokes?

Model Write the letters on guidelines on the chalkboard as you say the stroke descriptions. Invite volunteers to use colored chalk to trace your letters as you repeat the stroke descriptions.

Corrective Strategy

To check letter width, write **x** or **X** and enclose it in a rectangle.

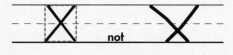

2 Write and Evaluate

After students have practiced writing the letters on marker boards or slates or on other paper, ask them to trace and write each letter on the page. Remind students to take time to write each letter carefully.

Stop and Check To help students evaluate, ask:

- Do your slant strokes in **x** cross about halfway between the midline and the baseline?
- Do the slant strokes in your **X** cross near the midline?
- Do your two slant strokes in **k** meet about halfway between the midline and baseline?
- Do your two slant strokes in **K** meet near the midline?
- Does your **z** begin on the midline?
- Is the second slide right stroke in your **Z** on the baseline?

3 Apply

Before students write words to complete the page, call attention to the vertical slant of the letters. Point out that manuscript is very easy to read because it is vertical. For this reason, it is often used for signs and labels. After students write, guide them in completing the direction in the Key feature at the bottom of the page.

PRACTICE MASTER 8

Manuscript Review

Write the letters.
x x x x   X X X X
k k k k   K K K K
z z z z   Z Z Z Z

Write the words.
exit   flex   knight
ticket   fuzzy   amaze
Xeres   Xanthos   Karen
Kevin   Zach   Zurich

Practice Master 8   Copyright © Zaner-Bloser, Inc.

Practice

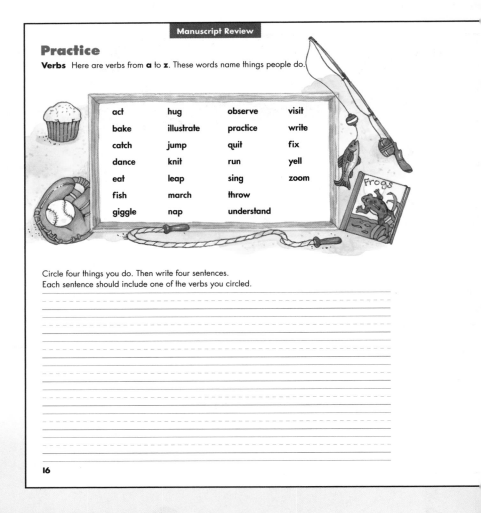

Practice

Verbs Here are verbs from **a** to **z**. These words name things people do.

act	hug	observe	visit
bake	illustrate	practice	write
catch	jump	quit	fix
dance	knit	run	yell
eat	leap	sing	zoom
fish	march	throw	
giggle	nap	understand	

Circle four things you do. Then write four sentences.
Each sentence should include one of the verbs you circled.

16

Review

Direct the students to look at the verbs, or action words, in the box on student page 16. Point out that all the letters of the lowercase alphabet are included. Ask them to describe what they remember about the shape, size, spacing, and slant of letters and words written in manuscript.

Review the stroke descriptions and model again any of the letters the students may be having difficulty writing.

Ask a volunteer to give a verbal description of one of the letters. Challenge the other students to identify the letter being described and then write it on guidelines on the chalkboard.

Write and Evaluate

Have the students write the sentences on student page 16, remembering to form the letters carefully so they will be legible.

 Stop and Check To help students evaluate their writing, ask:

- Did you write with correct strokes so your letters have good shape?
- Did you use the guidelines to help make letters with correct size?
- Do your short letters touch both the midline and the baseline?
- Do your tall letters touch both the headline and the baseline?
- Do your short letters with descenders touch the headline of the next writing space?
- Are your letters written with good vertical slant?

Corrective Strategy

The slide right and slide left strokes are the same width.

Z not Z

Note: To strengthen visual and motor skills while students are using manuscript writing, provide graph paper and ask students to write spelling words vertically and horizontally, one letter per square. Surrounding squares can then be filled with other letters to create a word search puzzle for a partner to solve.

Application

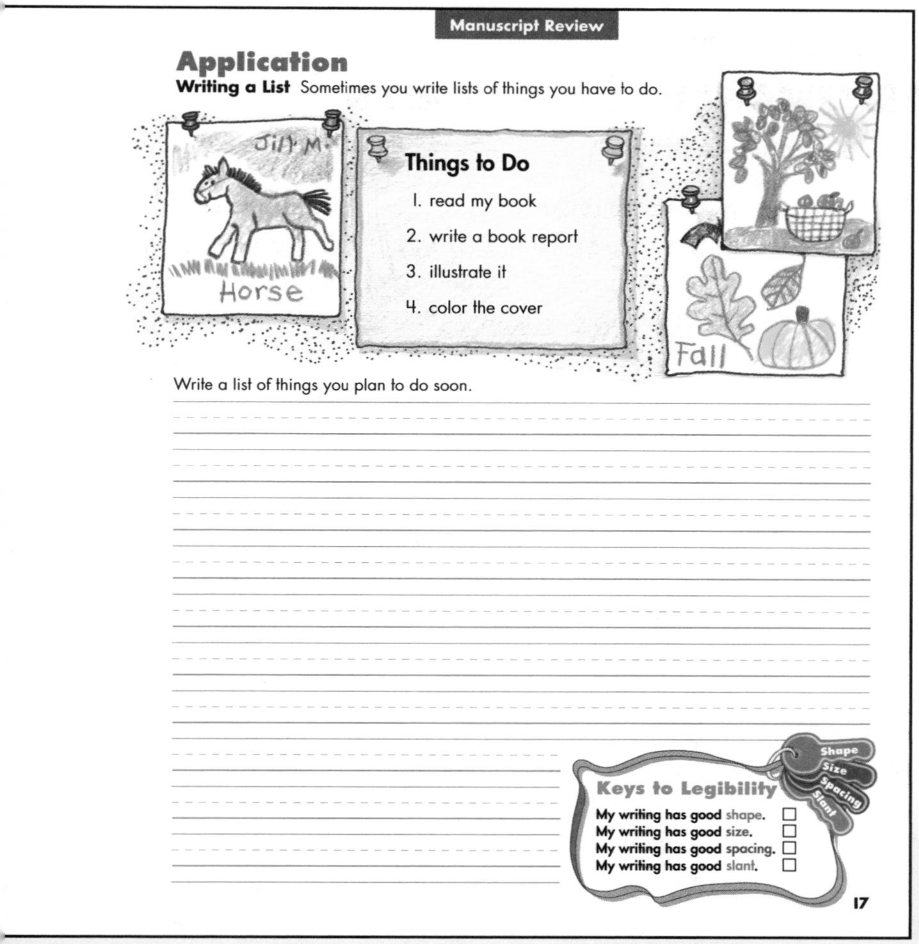

Writing a List Sometimes you write lists of things you have to do.

Things to Do

1. read my book
2. write a book report
3. illustrate it
4. color the cover

Write a list of things you plan to do soon.

Keys to Legibility

My writing has good shape. ☐
My writing has good size. ☐
My writing has good spacing. ☐
My writing has good slant. ☐

17

Application

More About Practice

Handwriting practice is most beneficial when it is done in the student's primary modality. Auditory learners can take turns saying stroke descriptions for each other to write. Visual learners might use colored chalk to highlight specific strokes in a letter. Kinesthetic learners will enjoy using their finger to trace letters on a tactile surface, such as sandpaper.

Apply

Read the list on student page 17 aloud with the students. Brainstorm possible items for a list, and write several on the chalkboard. Then have the students write their own lists. Remind them to write carefully and to use the guidelines to help them form letters and words that are legible.

Coaching Hint

Practice When students practice the writing skills they have learned in practical ways, they come to see the importance of writing. To reinforce manuscript writing throughout the year, have students do many different kinds of writing. Activities may include the following:

- Label pictures and objects.
- Make lists of things in categories.
- Write invitations.
- Write about field trips.
- Write facts.
- Retell a story in writing.
- Write about books.
- Write stories, poems, and descriptions.

Phonics

Rhyming Words, pp. T18, T20 In addition to hearing rhyming words, students need to see the words in print. Write the poem on student page 18 on the board. Read the poem aloud, pointing to each word as you say it. Explain that many poems contain words that rhyme. Rhyming words have the same ending sounds. Circle the rhyming words. Read the poem again, and emphasize the ending sounds of the rhyming words: *white/night* and *sea/me.* Invite students to repeat these words after you. Isolate the sounds that form the rhyme (**-ite, -ee**). Have students repeat these sounds.

Beginner/Emergent Speakers: Print rhyming words from the unit (*white/night, sea/me,* and *good/should*) in bold print on index cards. Shuffle the cards and place them in rows. Have students match pairs of rhyming words.

Intermediate/Fluent Speakers: On the board, list pairs of rhyming words from the unit. Use the words to create colored rhyme chains. Write one of the words on a strip of colored paper. Loop the strip and glue the ends to form the first link in the chain. Read the word on the loop aloud and ask students to identify the word in the list that rhymes with it. Write the rhyming word on a strip of paper that is the same color as the first loop. Brainstorm other words that rhyme with the words in the chain. Ask students to write these words on strips of paper and add them to the chain. Create rhyme chains for the other words in the list. Use a different color of paper for each chain.

Vocabulary Development

Sports Names, p. T25 Teach students the names of popular American sports. Show pictures of athletes playing each sport. If possible, bring in some of the items used to play the sports listed on student page 25. (If these items are unavailable, highlight each piece of equipment in pictures to reinforce the meaning of the sports terms.) Write the name of the sport on the board in both manuscript and cursive writing. Point to the name of each sport as you present the appropriate pictures and/or equipment. Use vivid descriptive words and phrases. Encourage students to share their experiences with each sport.

Beginner/Emergent Speakers: Have students play a memory game. Create two sets of illustrated word cards. On the first set, write in manuscript the name of each sport. Add an illustration or photograph to the card. On the second set, write the name of each sport in cursive. Add the same illustration or photo that you used on the manuscript cards. Tell students to match manuscript and cursive cards.

Intermediate Speakers: Have students write an original sentence about one of the sports listed on student page 25. Invite students to share their work with the class.

Advanced/Fluent Speakers: Have students create riddles about the sports listed on student page 25. For example, students might say, *I am played with a small ball and a racquet. What sport am I?*

Specific Teaching Tips

In this unit, students begin the transition from manuscript to cursive writing. Keep in mind that some students may have learned to write in cursive only and may need more guidance in forming manuscript letters. Others may be unfamiliar with the Roman alphabet and may need extra assistance with both manuscript and cursive forms. As you introduce a letter in cursive, model the manuscript form as well. Help students see that several letters are similar in shape in manuscript and cursive. Help students make the connection that a cursive letter shaped like its manuscript counterpart will require similar hand movements for its formation.

Coaching Hint

Letter Scramble, p. T23 If students find this activity confusing, modify it in the following ways, using cursive and manuscript letter flashcards.

Beginner/Emergent Speakers: Place one cursive card and two or three manuscript cards (make sure one of these matches the cursive card) face-up on the student's desk. Have the student match the cursive letter card to its corresponding manuscript card.

Intermediate and Advanced/Fluent Speakers: Have partners play a matching game, such as "Go Fish." Shuffle the manuscript and cursive letter cards together. Deal seven cards to each player and place the remaining cards face down on the desk between them. Partners will take turns asking each other for script or cursive letter cards, hoping to make a match. If a player cannot make a match, that player draws a card from the pile and the play goes to the player's partner. Matches are made when corresponding script and cursive cards are paired. Model the method of play with questions such as, "Do you have the manuscript **B**? Do you have the cursive **G**?"

Reading Cursive Writing, p. T24

Reading cursive letters can be a challenge for many students. Some may have learned to write in a cursive form that differs from that taught in this program. Others may be unfamiliar with the Roman alphabet and cursive forms. You may need to spend time helping students distinguish between the letters **o, p, b,** and **d**; as well as **p, g,** and **q**. Also, anticipate helping students distinguish between **l, t** and **k; n** and **m; u, v,** and **w;** and **y** and **g**.

Keys to Legibility

Shape, Size, Spacing, Slant, p. T32 Help students understand what the Keys to Legibility mean. Write a sentence on the board and read it aloud. Then use it to focus on each key.

Shape Explain that letters have shapes. Draw a circle on the board and have students compare it to letters in your sentence. Which letters have a circular shape? Point out other letter shapes in your sentence.

Size Ask students to identify the tall letters in your sentence. Then ask them to identify the small letters.

Spacing Have two students stand next to each other. Point to the space between them and say, "This is a small space." Gesture the meaning by placing your hands close together. Tell students that the space between letters in a word is small. Show examples in your sentence.

Have two other students stand farther apart from each other. Say, "This is a big space." Gesture the meaning by placing your hands far apart. Tell students that the space between words in a sentence is big. Show examples in your sentence.

Slant Draw a straight vertical line on the board and say, "This line is vertical." Gesture the meaning of *vertical* with your hands. Have students practice saying the word. Draw a slanted line on the board and say, "This line is slanted." Write some letters on the board that have no slant and others that have an appropriate slant. Tell students that letters with good slant are easy to read.

CULTURAL NOTES

Poetry can help students understand and appreciate such nuances of the English language as phonemes and graphemes, vocabulary, and figurative language. Before students engage in poetry analysis or appreciation, explain any cultural references or figurative language in the poem that could impede understanding.

Pretest

I'd Like To Be a Lighthouse

I'd like to be a lighthouse
 And scrubbed and painted white.
I'd like to be a lighthouse
 And stay awake all night
To keep my eye on everything
 That sails my patch of sea;
I'd like to be a lighthouse
 With the ships all watching me.

Rachel Field

18

Getting Started

Explain to the students that during handwriting time, they will be learning to write the letters of the alphabet and the numerals in cursive writing.

Point out the poem by Rachel Field on student page 18, and read it aloud with the students. Tell them that Field was an American writer who lived in the early half of the 20th century. She wrote many children's books, poetry, and plays as well as works for adults.

Direct students to notice the writing guidelines on student page 19. Explain that this is where they will write the poem, using their best handwriting. Ask them to keep their pretests in their writing portfolios for comparison with their posttests later in the year. You may want the students to write the pretest periodically to provide samples of their improvement. Students who learned cursive handwriting in second grade may choose to write the pretest in cursive.

Write the title and the poem in your best handwriting.

19

Evaluate

Observe the students as they write the poem. Note that many may still be using manuscript writing some or all of the time. Use this page as a pretest to help you assess each student's current handwriting skills.

Coaching Hint

Hands-On Writing Use tagboard or self-adhesive ruled name strips to make a desktop nametag for each student in your class. Tape the nametags to the students' desks so they can use them as writing models. (visual)

Right Hand/Left Hand
To increase awareness of left-handedness, explain that left-handers make up 10–15% of the population. Famous "left-ies" include Ronald Reagan, Benjamin Franklin, Albert Einstein, Oprah Winfrey, soccer star Pelé, and baseball greats Sandy Koufax and Babe Ruth. In some sports, such as baseball, left-handedness is sometimes considered to be an advantage. (auditory)

Self-Evaluation

Self-evaluation is an important step in the handwriting process. By identifying their own strengths and weaknesses, students become independent learners. The steps in the self-evaluation process are as follows:

1. Question
Students should ask themselves questions such as these: "Is my slant correct?" "Do my letters rest on the baseline?" Teacher modeling is vital in teaching effective questioning techniques.

2. Compare
Students should compare their handwriting to correct models.

3. Evaluate
Students should determine strengths and weaknesses in their handwriting based on the Keys to Legibility.

4. Diagnose
Students should diagnose the cause of any difficulties. Possible causes include incorrect paper or pencil position, inconsistent pressure on the writing implement, and incorrect strokes.

5. Improve
Self-evaluation should include a means of improvement through additional instruction and continued practice.

Note: Zaner-Bloser's *Evaluation Guide* for grade 3 handwriting is a handy tool for evaluating students' writing. The evaluation criteria are the Keys to Legibility. Samples of students' handwriting, ranging in quality from excellent to poor, provide helpful comparison for evaluation.

Welcome to Cursive

You are writing very well.
Your manuscript letters look good.
Each letter stands straight up and down,
The way manuscript letters should.

You're ready to write a new way.
You're ready for cursive, at last!
Cursive writing is graceful,
Cursive writing is fast.

20

Welcome to Cursive

Encourage volunteers to read aloud the poem on student page 20. Invite discussion on likenesses and differences they have already noticed between manuscript and cursive writing.

Initiate class discussion of how the students have seen cursive handwriting used. Ask how they have observed adults use cursive writing.

Work through student page 21 with the students, and have them respond to the writing prompts on the page.

You are ready for cursive writing! As you begin, you will notice how cursive writing is different from manuscript writing. Look at these words.

ready   ready

Notice that the letters in the cursive word are joined together.

Notice that cursive writing slants forward.

Try it. Write some letters you know in cursive.

What else can you write in cursive? Write it here.

The pages in this book will help you learn to write cursive letters, words, and sentences.

Let's go!

21

Introducing Cursive

The following are some criteria to help determine whether students are ready for cursive writing.

Reading Level Does the student show reading proficiency near grade level?

Manuscript Mastery Is the student able to write legibly in manuscript?

Cursive Letter Recognition Is the student able to recognize and identify all cursive letters?

Cursive Word Reading Is the student able to read cursive words, understanding that letters preceded by **b, o, v,** and **w** are written slightly differently?

Grouping of Letters Is the student able to group letters according to size, shape, beginning stroke, and ending stroke?

Understanding of Terminology Does the student understand the terms for cursive handwriting?

Understanding of Slant Does the student understand that slant is determined by paper position, the direction in which the downstrokes are pulled, and the shifting of the paper as the writing space is filled?

Cursive Letters and Numerals

Circle the uppercase cursive letters that are your initials.
Underline the lowercase cursive letters that are in your name.
Draw a box around the uppercase cursive letter that begins the name of your state.

Now take a closer look.
Which manuscript and cursive letters are most alike? Draw stars beside them.

Aa Bb Cc Dd Ee Ff Gg

Aa Bb Cc Dd Ee Ff Gg

Hh Ii Jj Kk Ll Mm

Hh Ii Jj Kk Ll Mm

22

Cursive Letters and Numerals

Students can use the chart on these two pages as a reference resource to identify lowercase and uppercase cursive letters and numerals.

Assist the students as needed in reading and following the directions on student pages 22 and 23. Invite discussion on which manuscript and cursive letters are most alike and most different.

Practice Master 11 *is available for use with these pages.*

Circle the cursive numeral that tells your age.

23

Review the Lines

Review with students the use of guidelines for correct letter formation. Draw guidelines on the chalkboard, using colored chalk to identify the headline, midline, and baseline. Invite volunteers to write words on the guidelines.

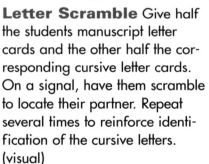

Coaching Hint

Letter Scramble Give half the students manuscript letter cards and the other half the corresponding cursive letter cards. On a signal, have them scramble to locate their partner. Repeat several times to reinforce identification of the cursive letters. (visual)

Reading Cursive Writing

Look at the orange manuscript lowercase letter.
Circle the cursive lowercase letter that matches it.

a	a	b	c	d	e	f
g	d	e	f	g	h	i
n	j	k	l	m	n	o
r	p	q	r	s	t	u
z	u	v	w	x	y	z

Look at the orange manuscript uppercase letter.
Circle the cursive uppercase letter that matches it.

B	A	B	C	D	E	F
E	D	E	F	G	H	I
M	I	J	K	L	M	N
Q	O	P	Q	R	S	T
Y	U	V	W	X	Y	Z

24

Reading Cursive Writing

Assist the students as needed in reading and following the directions on student page 24.

Poll students to find out which cursive letters and numerals are most difficult for them to read. Discuss possible reasons for this difficulty. Then ask students to describe similarities and differences between manuscript and cursive letters and numerals.

Read the name of a sport written in manuscript.
Circle the matching word written in cursive.

baseball	*baseball*	*football*	*soccer*
volleyball	*diving*	*volleyball*	*skating*
tennis	*hockey*	*skiing*	*tennis*
football	*football*	*hockey*	*basketball*
skating	*swimming*	*skating*	*tennis*

Read the name of a sport written in cursive.
Write the name in manuscript.

tennis

basketball

soccer

ice skating

25

Assist the students as needed in reading and following the directions on student page 25.

Ask students to describe the similarities and differences between the cursive words they read and the manuscript words they wrote.

Coaching Hint

Evaluation Encourage students to look through their writing folders or other school papers and select a sample that best showcases their ability to write legibly. Students may change their selections as their handwriting skills improve. (visual, kinesthetic)

Left-Handed Writers
Right-Handed Writers

Suggest that students refer to these pages throughout the year as a reminder of proper posture and correct paper and pencil position. Demonstrate correct positions for both left-handed and right-handed writers. Then ask students to place a sheet of paper in the proper position on their desks, pick up a pencil, and write their names.

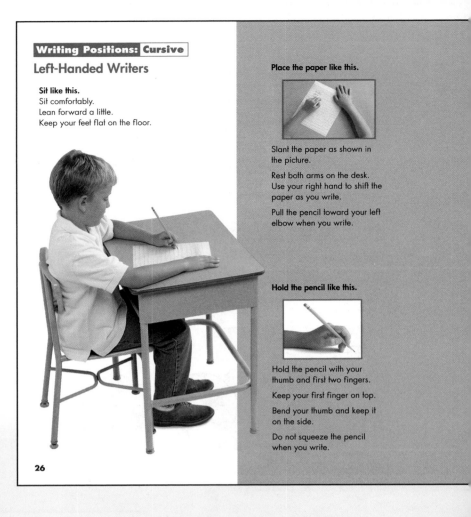

Writing Positions: Cursive
Left-Handed Writers

Sit like this.
Sit comfortably.
Lean forward a little.
Keep your feet flat on the floor.

Place the paper like this.

Slant the paper as shown in the picture.

Rest both arms on the desk. Use your right hand to shift the paper as you write.

Pull the pencil toward your left elbow when you write.

Hold the pencil like this.

Hold the pencil with your thumb and first two fingers.

Keep your first finger on top.

Bend your thumb and keep it on the side.

Do not squeeze the pencil when you write.

26

Writing Positions:
Cursive

Sitting Position

Using correct body position when writing will help students write better letters. They will also not tire as quickly. Encourage them to sit comfortably erect with their feet flat on the floor and their hips touching the back of the chair. Both arms should rest on the desk. Be sure students are relaxed, holding their pencils correctly.

Paper Position

Correct paper placement is a critical factor in legibility. To ensure that the paper is placed correctly for both right- and left-handed students, use tape to form a frame on the desk so the students will be able to place the paper in the correct position.

Left-Handed Writers

Right-Handed Writers

Pencil Position

Model good pencil position for the students. The writing implement is held between the thumb and the first two fingers, about an inch above the point. The first finger rests on top of the implement. The end of the bent thumb is placed against the writing instrument to hold it high in the hand and near the knuckle.

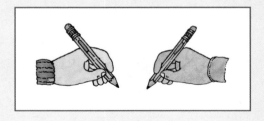

See the **Handwriting Positions Wall Chart** *for more information.*

Practice Masters 9–10 *provide more information on handwriting positions.*

T26

Right-Handed Writers

Sit like this.
Sit comfortably.
Lean forward a little.
Keep your feet flat on the floor.

Place the paper like this.

Slant the paper as shown in the picture.

Rest both arms on the desk. Use your left hand to shift the paper as you write.

Pull the pencil toward the middle of your body when you write.

Hold the pencil like this.

Hold the pencil with your thumb and first two fingers.

Keep your first finger on top.

Bend your thumb and keep it on the side.

Do not squeeze the pencil when you write.

27

Note: Writing on a slanted surface provides stability to the base of the hand and can help students maintain good hand and wrist position. To make a slanted surface, position a three-ring binder sideways on a student's desktop. The slanted cover of the binder provides a surface for writing. Use a binder clip or a small piece of tape to secure the student's paper to one side of the binder.

Special Helps
Maureen King
Occupational Therapist

If a student uses a clenched grip on the writing implement, or if the writer's fingers or thumb joints turn white while writing, try this activity. Provide a toy such as a Magna Doodle or an Etch-a-Sketch. Have the student work with the toy mounted upside down at shoulder height on a vertical surface, such as a wall, an easel, or standing in the chalk tray of the chalkboard. As the student operates the toy, he or she will have to reach a little higher than usual, promoting development of the whole arm, shoulder to wrist for the interaction needed to hold and use a writing implement efficiently.

Coaching Hints

Pencil Position The Zaner-Bloser *Writing Frame* can be used to show good hand position for both left-handed and right-handed writers because the hand holding the pencil and resting over the frame automatically settles into the correct position. (kinesthetic)

Pencil Position Many students hold their pencils too close to the point. To help students position their fingers on the pencil, demonstrate how to wrap a rubber band tightly around the pencil at least an inch away from the point. Explain that the rubber band shows where to hold the pencil and keeps the fingers from slipping. (kinesthetic)

Alternate Position Students who have difficulty with the traditional pencil position may prefer the alternate method of holding the pencil between the first and second fingers. (kinesthetic)

Left-Handed Writers Give left-handed students the opportunity to write at the chalkboard where they will have greater freedom of arm movement until they have learned correct letter formation. (kinesthetic)

Basic Strokes

Undercurve

The undercurve is one of the basic strokes used to write cursive letters.

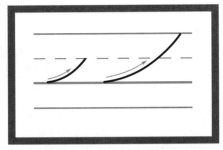

Undercurve Stroke Description:
Touch the baseline; curve under and up to the midline (or headline).

Basic Strokes
Undercurve
An **undercurve** is one of the basic strokes used to write cursive letters.

An undercurve stroke swings up.

Trace an undercurve stroke at the beginning of each lowercase letter.

b e f h i j k
l p r s t u w

Trace an undercurve stroke at the beginning of each uppercase letter.

B G L P R S

Trace and write undercurve strokes.

28

Coaching Hint

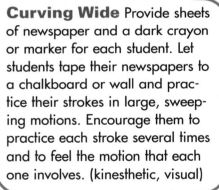

Curving Wide Provide sheets of newspaper and a dark crayon or marker for each student. Let students tape their newspapers to a chalkboard or wall and practice their strokes in large, sweeping motions. Encourage them to practice each stroke several times and to feel the motion that each one involves. (kinesthetic, visual)

Present the Stroke

Direct students to look at the stroke models and the photo on student page 28. Explain that there are four basic strokes used in forming cursive letters. The undercurve stroke is one of them.

Have students read the directions and trace the strokes on the student page. If any students have difficulty identifying the stroke in a certain letter, model the letter on the chalkboard and highlight the undercurve stroke in a different color.

Trace and Write

Ask students to trace and write the two sizes of undercurve strokes on the student page. Remind them to begin each one at the starting dot.

 Stop and Check To help students evaluate their writing, ask:

- Did you begin each stroke at the correct starting point on the baseline?
- Did you end each short undercurve stroke at the midline?
- Does each of your tall undercurve strokes end at the headline?

Introduce this verse to help students remember the basic strokes in cursive writing.

Undercurves swing.   Undercurve, downcurve.
Downcurves dive.   Overcurve, slant.
Overcurves bounce.   As you write cursive letters,
Slants just slide.   Remember this chant.

Downcurve

A **downcurve** is one of the basic strokes used to write cursive letters.

A downcurve stroke dives down.

Trace a downcurve stroke at the beginning of each lowercase letter.

a   c   d   g   o   q

Trace a downcurve stroke at the beginning of each uppercase letter.

A   C   D   E   O

Trace and write downcurve strokes.

29

Downcurve

A downcurve is one of the basic strokes used to write cursive letters.

Downcurve Stroke Description:
Touch the midline (or headline); curve left and down to the baseline.

Present the Stroke

Direct students to look at the stroke models and the photo on student page 29. Explain that the downcurve stroke is another basic stroke used to write cursive letters.

Have students read the directions and trace the strokes on the student page. If any students have difficulty identifying the stroke in a certain letter, model the letter on the chalkboard and highlight the downcurve stroke in a different color.

Trace and Write

Ask students to trace and write the two sizes of downcurve strokes on the student page. Remind them to begin each one at the starting dot.

✓ **Stop and Check** To help students evaluate their writing, ask:

• Did you begin each short downcurve stroke near the midline?
• Does each of your tall downcurve strokes begin near the headline?
• Do your downcurve strokes end at the baseline?

PRACTICE MASTERS 12–13

Basic Strokes

Overcurve

The overcurve is one of the basic strokes used to write cursive letters.

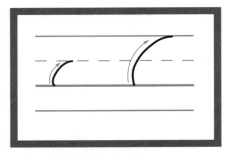

Overcurve Stroke Description:
Touch the baseline; curve up and right to the midline (or headline).

Basic Strokes
Overcurve

An **overcurve** is one of the basic strokes used to write cursive letters.

An overcurve stroke bounces up.

Trace an overcurve stroke at the beginning of each lowercase letter.

m   n   v   x   y   z

Trace an overcurve stroke at the beginning of each uppercase letter.

L   J   Q

Trace and write overcurve strokes.

30

Coaching Hint

Basic Strokes For students who need additional practice with basic strokes, give each student a card on which one of the cursive basic strokes (undercurve, downcurve, overcurve, slant) is written. Tell students to write that stroke on lined paper and then to identify all the uppercase and lowercase letters that contain that stroke. Students can trade cards and repeat the activity. (visual, kinesthetic)

Present the Stroke

Direct students to look at the stroke models and the photo on student page 30. Explain that the overcurve is another basic stroke used to write cursive letters.

Have students read the directions and trace the strokes on the student page. If any students have difficulty identifying the stroke in a certain letter, model the letter on the chalkboard and highlight the overcurve stroke in a different color.

Trace and Write

Ask students to trace and write the two sizes of overcurve strokes on the student page. Remind them to begin each one at the starting dot.

✓ **Stop and Check** To help students evaluate their writing, ask:

- Did you begin each stroke at the correct starting point on the baseline?
- Did you end each short overcurve stroke near the midline?
- Does each of your tall overcurve strokes end near the headline?

Slant

A **slant** is one of the basic strokes used to write cursive letters.

A slant stroke slides.

/   /

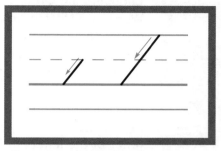

Trace a slant stroke in each lowercase letter.

a   b   d   f   g   h   i

j   k   l   m   t   u   y

Trace a slant stroke in each uppercase letter.

A   B   K   P   R   U   X   Y

Trace and write slant strokes.

/   /   /   /   /   /   /   /

✓

/   /   /   /   /   /

✓

31

Slant

A slant is one of the basic strokes used to write cursive letters.

Slant Stroke Description:
Touch the midline (or headline); slant left to the baseline.

Present the Stroke

Direct students to look at the stroke models and the photo on student page 31. Explain that the slant stroke is another basic stroke used to write cursive letters.

Have students read the directions and trace the strokes on the student page. If any students have difficulty identifying the stroke in a certain letter, model the letter on the chalkboard and highlight the slant stroke in a different color.

Trace and Write

Ask students to trace and write the two sizes of slant strokes on the student page. Remind them to begin each one at the starting dot.

✓ **Stop and Check** To help students evaluate their writing, ask:

- Did you begin each short slant stroke at the midline?
- Does each of your tall slant strokes begin at the headline?
- Do your slant strokes end at the baseline?

PRACTICE MASTERS 14–15

Making Sense of Directions

Changing the Order of Letters to Write a New Word, p. T75 This activity will challenge students' understanding of vocabulary, recognition of high-frequency words, and knowledge of English spelling patterns. Assist students by using letter tiles, or a set of letter cards that you made, to form one of the words listed on student page 75. Then manipulate the tiles, changing the order of the letters to form a new word. Help students see that the letters in both words are the same, but the order is different.

Intermediate and Advanced/Fluent Speakers: Organize students in pairs. Give each pair letter tiles or letter cards and a dictionary. Call out one of the words listed on student page 75. Have partners form the word with their letter tiles or cards. Then, instruct students to manipulate the tiles, changing the order of the letters to form a new word. Partners can check the dictionary to confirm that the rearranged letters form an actual word.

Vocabulary Development

Words That Name Breakfast Foods, p. T60 Provide the foods (or pictures of the foods) listed on student page 37. If possible, give students samples to touch, taste, and smell. Use a similar process when teaching the names of vegetables on student page 61. (Before sharing food, check for food allergies and cultural taboos.)

Intermediate and Advanced/Fluent Speakers: Use words that name vegetables and breakfast foods to help students express personal preferences. Teach expressions such as *I like, my favorite,* and *I dislike.* Use the vegetables and breakfast food names to make statements such as "I like carrots. I dislike eggs. Breakfast is my favorite meal." Then, have students take classroom surveys, polling each other about breakfast foods and vegetables. Encourage students to graph their results.

Time Words, p. T63 Write the times from Sam's schedule on the board. Read each time aloud as you point to its written form. Explain that an activity occurs at each of the given times. Use realia, pictures, or pantomime to explain Sam's activities. Help students create a schedule of their own typical school day. Write times in one column on the board. List activities in a second column. Ask students to match the times to the activities. Be sure to have students practice the time words.

Intermediate and Advanced/Fluent Speakers: Distribute blank bingo cards. Write a list of times on the board. Have students fill in their bingo grids—except for the free space in the center—with listed times. Call out each time from the list. When students have a called time written on their card, have them cover it with a counter or a piece of scrap paper. When a student believes he or she has a winning sequence, ask that student to read back the times covered on his or her bingo card. This game also provides an opportunity to review the terms *horizontal, vertical,* and *diagonal.*

Specific Teaching Tips

Cursive writing requires hand movements with which some students may be unfamiliar. Demonstrate how to join the end of one letter to the start of another. First, model common letter combinations, such as **ch, ta, nt, th,** and **et.** Use a Think Aloud to describe your method. For example, write the cursive letters **c** and **h** on the board. Point to the end of the curve in the letter **c.** Say, "The joining of these letters begins here." Draw a line joining the **c** to the **h.** Say, "From the end of the **c,** the line curves up to the top of the **h.**" Describe the shape and hand movements you use. Check students' progress as they repeat the action.

English-Language Learners

ELL TIPS

Fun and Games

Tall or Short? p. T33 Students may recognize the descriptors *tall* and *short,* but they may not know that these words can describe letters. To review these descriptors, place pictures illustrating *tall* and *short* on the board. Point to the *tall* picture and say "tall." Point to the *short* picture and say "short." Look around the room for more examples of *tall* and *short.*

After reviewing the meanings of *tall* and *short,* help students use the words to classify letters. Show students letter cards for **b, h, l,** and **k.** When you present each card, say, "This is the letter_____. It is a tall letter." Show students letter cards for **c, e, g, j,** and **m.** When you present each card, say, "This is the letter ____. It is a short letter."

Coaching Hint

Positions for Writing, p. T44 Before teaching this self-corrective strategy, explain what it means to freeze. Point out that *freeze* has more than one meaning. It can refer to water and other liquids and mean "to become solid by loss of heat." It can also refer to people and other animals and mean "to stop what you are doing and remain perfectly still."

Help students make the connection between *freeze* and *frozen.* Explain that when something is frozen, it is like a statue and cannot move. Strike a statue-like pose as you say, "Freeze!"

Write Away

Jokes and Riddles, p. T77 Take advantage of the value that wordplay—games, riddles, and jokes—has in learning new vocabulary. At the same time, realize that jokes and riddles often require an understanding of figurative language or cultural background that students may not possess. While telling jokes and asking riddles can enhance understanding of word meaning, they can also intimidate some students who may find themselves unable to understand the joke or figure out the riddle.

Special Helps

Connect Four, p. T73 Use this game to reinforce the meaning of directional terms, such as *horizontal, vertical,* and *slant.* Review these terms and then model rules for play. Explain that the winner will have four game pieces in a row. Game pieces may be arranged vertically, horizontally, or on a slant (diagonally). Draw circles on the board to represent the different winning arrangements.

CULTURAL NOTES

Students who have learned a language with a nonalphabetic writing system (such as Chinese) or a non-Roman writing system (such as Russian) will benefit from a review of the complete Roman alphabet before you review numerals. Students will also benefit from listening to pronunciation models so that they will recognize the name and pronunciation of each letter when it is used in class.

Writing Lowercase Letters

Keys to Legibility

Explain to students that good handwriting is legible handwriting. The most important thing to remember is that readers must be able to read a message in order to understand its meaning.

Brainstorm with students qualities of legible handwriting. Write responses on the chalkboard. These might include neatness, carefully written letters, and letters that are not too crowded.

Point out that there are four Keys to Legibility. They are easy to remember because they all start with **s**: **shape, size, spacing,** and **slant**.

Explain that **shape** describes the strokes that form each letter and give it a unique appearance. **Size** describes the height of letters. **Spacing** describes the space between letters, words, and sentences. **Slant** refers to the angle of writing on the paper. Using these keys will help the students improve the legibility of their writing.

Use the **Keys to Legibility Wall Chart** *for more information.*

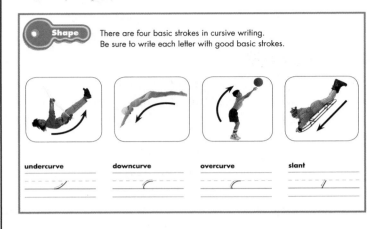

Keys to Legibility

You will learn to write lowercase cursive letters. As you write, pay attention to the four keys to legibility.

Shape There are four basic strokes in cursive writing. Be sure to write each letter with good basic strokes.

undercurve   downcurve   overcurve   slant

Circle each letter that has an undercurve beginning.

w   d   c   h   w

Circle each letter that has a downcurve beginning.

a   j   p   g   s

Circle each letter that has an overcurve beginning.

b   n   r   v   z

Circle each letter that has a slant stroke.

c   k   l   m   o

32

Present the Key

Point out to students that the basic strokes they learned in the previous pages are the basis for a letter's shape.

Read and discuss with students the information and illustrations in the box on student page 32. Then help them as needed as they complete the activity at the bottom of the page.

Coaching Hint

Hands-On Writing Use the overhead projector to project a letter onto the chalkboard. Ask students to wet their index finger in a cup of water and trace over the stroke you name. (visual, auditory, kinesthetic)

Present the Key

Read and discuss the information and illustration in the box on student page 33. Emphasize that writing letters on guidelines fosters letters of consistent size. Then help students as needed as they read the directions and complete the activity at the bottom of the page.

Coaching Hint

Writing Lines Review with students the use of the guidelines for correct letter formation. As you demonstrate on the chalkboard, have students do the following on paper:

- Draw over the baseline with a red crayon.
- Draw over the headline and midline with a blue crayon.

(kinesthetic, visual, auditory)

Fun and Games

Tall or Short? Make a set of letter cards by writing uppercase and lowercase letters in cursive on paper with guidelines. Cut out each letter and tape it to an index card. Write "tall" and "short" on the chalkboard or on chart paper to form two columns. Ask students to select cards and tape them under the appropriate column.

Tall: all uppercase letters, **b, d, f, h, k, l, t**

Short: a, c, e, g, i, j, m, n, o, p, q, r, s, u, v, w, x, y, z

Ask students to tell how they know whether letters are tall or short. Remind them that tall letters touch the headline and short letters touch the midline. Invite volunteers to make a check mark beside cards with letters with descenders that go below the baseline and touch the next headline: **f, g, j, J, p, q, y, Y, z, Z.**

Place the letter cards in the writing center and invite students to sort them by size.

Keys to Legibility

Remind students that good hand-writing is legible handwriting. The most important thing to remember is that readers must be able to read a message in order to understand its meaning.

Review that **shape** describes the strokes that form each letter and give it a unique appearance. **Size** describes the height of letters. **Spacing** describes the space between letters, words, and sentences. **Slant** refers to the angle of writing on the paper. Using these Keys will help the students improve the legibility of their writing.

Keys to Legibility

To help make your lowercase cursive letters easy to read, pay attention to the four keys to legibility.

Spacing — Look at the spacing between letters and words.

There should be space for O between letters.

better spacing

There should be space for \ between words.

word spacing

Circle the word that has good letter spacing.

spacing   spacing   spacing

Circle the line that has good word spacing.

word spacing

word   spacing

word spacing

34

Present the Key

Point out to students that the space between letters, words, and sentences is a vital part of legibility.

Read and discuss with students the information and illustrations in the box on student page 34. Then help them as needed as they complete the activity at the bottom of the page.

Coaching Hint

Hands-On Writing On guidelines on the chalkboard, write words, singly or in pairs, with obvious errors in spacing. Challenge volunteers to come to the board, identify an error, and tell how it should be corrected. (visual, kinesthetic)

Write Away

Slant Guide Make guide sheets to help students write with good slant. Using a thick, dark-colored marker, write slant strokes across blank guidelines (see Practice Master 109) to fill a page. Leave a finger space between the strokes. Duplicate the page and give one copy to each student.

Encourage students to place the guide sheets under their papers as they write. The dark strokes should show through and provide a guide for writing with good slant. Invite volunteers to show writing samples with uniform slant. Ask them to tell how consistent slant helps make their writing legible.

Slant Look at the slant of your letters.

Cursive letters have a uniform forward slant.

forward slant

Circle a word that has good slant.

slant slant slant

To write with good slant:

POSITION • Check your paper position.
PULL • Pull your downstrokes in the proper direction.
SHIFT • Shift your paper as you write.

If you are left-handed . . .

pull toward your left elbow.

If you are right-handed . . .

pull toward your midsection.

35

Present the Key

Read and discuss the information and illustration in the box on student page 35. Emphasize that writing letters and words with consistent forward slant fosters legibility. Help students as needed as they read the directions and complete the activity in the middle of the page. Then go over the **Position/Pull/Shift** information.

Coaching Hint

Slant Write the same word on the chalkboard in cursive and in manuscript. Use parallel lines of colored chalk to highlight the difference between manuscript verticality and cursive slant. (visual)

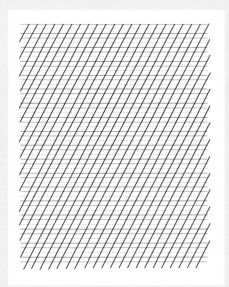

Featured Letters

i t u
w e l b
h f k r
s j p

Featured Keys to Legibility:

Shape
Size

Students will consider **shape** and **size** as they evaluate their writing.

Other Acceptable Letterforms

These are acceptable variations of the models in this book.

t k r
s p

Teaching the Letters:
Building Imagery

The purpose of the first step in teaching each letter is to help the students develop a clear **mental image** of the letter to be written. Appropriate questions about the letter help the students develop the image. The teacher is then asked to model, or demonstrate, the letter on the chalkboard, on large chart paper, or in the air, giving attention to the letter and its description, to establish **motor image**.

Write Undercurve Letters

i

You will learn to write these lowercase letters. Each letter begins with an undercurve stroke.

i   t   u   w   e   l   b
h   f   k   r   s   j   p

Trace and write undercurve strokes.

Keys to Legibility
Make your writing easy to read. As you write undercurve letters, you will pay attention to the shape and size of your writing.

Shape
Size

Remembering the four basic strokes will help you write letters with good shape.

undercurve   downcurve   overcurve   slant

Use the guidelines to help you write letters with good size.

l h   i w   p j

tall   short   letters with
letters   letters   descenders

36

---

1. Present the Letters

Point out the lowercase letters on the page, and explain that each one begins with an undercurve stroke. Encourage students to use their finger or a pencil to trace several of the undercurve strokes in these letters. Then have them trace and write the undercurve strokes on the guidelines.

Direct the students to notice the stop-and-check symbol at the end of the writing grids. Remind them that this symbol tells them to stop and check their writing. Then guide the students in circling their best undercurve stroke in each line.

2. Present the Keys

Point out the Key features on the student page. Explain to students that they will see these features often in the lessons that follow. The Keys help them consider certain qualities of their writing as they evaluate it.

What the research says ...

When teachers or other adults are asked to grade multiple versions of the same paper, differing only in handwriting quality, more neatly written papers receive higher marks for writing content than papers that are less legible.
—Steve Graham, *Handwriting Research and Resources: A Guide to Curriculum Planning*

Trace and write. Notice the undercurve beginning and ending.

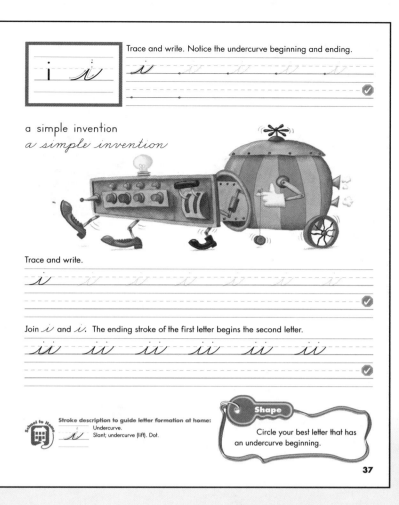

a simple invention
a simple invention

Trace and write.

Join *i* and *i*. The ending stroke of the first letter begins the second letter.

Shape
Circle your best letter that has an undercurve beginning.

37

- Undercurve
- Slant, undercurve, (lift)
- Dot

Coaching Hint

Instruction Time Students' progress in handwriting is greater when short, intensive periods of instruction are used, approximately fifteen minutes for a lesson.

---

1. Present the Letter

Help students focus on the letter **i** by asking:

- How many undercurve strokes are in **i**? *(two)*
- How does **i** end? *(with a dot)*

Model Write **i** on guidelines as you say the stroke description. Model writing **i** in the air as you repeat the stroke description. Have students say the description as they write **i** in the air with you.

Corrective Strategy

Pull the slant stroke toward the baseline; pause before the undercurve ending.

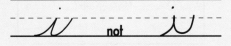

2. Write and Evaluate

After students have practiced writing **i** on scrap paper or practice boards, ask them to trace and write the first row of letters.

Stop and Check To help students evaluate **i,** ask:

- Does your first undercurve touch the midline?
- Does your ending stroke touch the midline?

School to Home

Families may use the stroke description on the student page to encourage good letter formation at home. **Practice Master 83** provides take-home practice for the letters **i** and **t**.

3. Apply

Ask students to complete the page by writing **i** and joining it to other letters. Remind students that the shape of a letter is determined by correctly written strokes.

PRACTICE MASTER 21

- Undercurve
- Slant, undercurve, (lift)
- Slide right

Trace and write.

letter time
letter time

Trace and write.

Join *t* and other letters. Notice the undercurve to undercurve joinings.

it it it it it it

tt tt tt ti ti ti

Shape
Circle your best letter that has an undercurve ending.

38

Coaching Hint

Left-Handed Writers Group left-handed students together for handwriting lessons if you can do so without calling attention to the practice. Left-handers will be able to see better when they are seated to the left of the chalkboard. (visual)

---

1. Present the Letter

Help students focus on the letter **t** by asking:
- What stroke follows the slant? *(undercurve)*
- How does **t** end? *(with a slide right)*

Model Write **t** on guidelines as you say the stroke description. Model writing **t** in the air as you repeat the stroke description. Have students say the words as they use their index finger to write **t** on their desktop.

Corrective Strategy
Swing wide on the undercurve to undercurve joining.

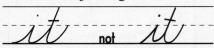

it not *it*

2. Write and Evaluate

After students have practiced writing **t** on scrap paper or practice boards, ask them to trace and write the first row of letters.

✓ **Stop and Check** To help students evaluate **t,** ask:
- Does your first undercurve end at the headline?
- Is your slant stroke pulled toward the baseline?

School to Home

Families may use the stroke description on the student page to encourage good letter formation at home. **Practice Master 83** provides take-home practice for the letters **i** and **t**.

3. Apply

Ask students to complete the page by writing **t** and joining it to other letters. Remind students to write carefully so their letters have correct shape.

PRACTICE MASTER 22

Trace and write.

u 𝓊

up in the clouds
up in the clouds

Trace and write.

Join 𝓊 and other letters. Notice the undercurve to undercurve joinings.

ut   ui   uit   iu   tu

tutu   tutu   tutu

Stroke description to guide letter formation at home:
Undercurve. Slant; undercurve.
Slant; undercurve.

Shape
Circle your best letter that has a slant stroke.

39

- Undercurve
- Slant, undercurve
- Slant, undercurve

Coaching Hint

Letter Practice Slates are great for letter practice. After you have modeled a letter, ask students to write on their slates or marker boards before they write in their books or on paper. (visual, kinesthetic)

---

1. Present the Letter

Help students focus on the letter **u** by asking:
- What stroke follows the first slant? *(undercurve)*
- How does **u** end? *(with an undercurve)*

Model Write **u** on guidelines as you say the stroke description. Model writing **u** in the air as you repeat the stroke description. Have students say the description as they write **u** in the air with you.

Corrective Strategy

Pause at the midline before writing the slant strokes.

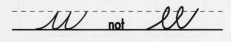

2. Write and Evaluate

After students have practiced writing **u** on scrap paper or practice boards, ask them to trace and write the first row of letters.

 Stop and Check To help students evaluate **u**, ask:
- Does your **u** begin at the baseline?
- Does your **u** end at the midline?

School to Home

Families may use the stroke description on the student page to encourage good letter formation at home. **Practice Master 84** provides take-home practice for the letters **u** and **w**.

3. Apply

Ask students to complete the page by writing **u** and joining it to other letters. Point out the helpfulness of comparing the shape of their letters with the models.

PRACTICE MASTER 23

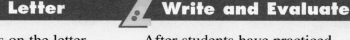

- Undercurve
- Slant, undercurve
- Slant, undercurve
- Checkstroke

Coaching Hint

Sitting Position Assign chairs, tables, and desks of varying heights to achieve the best fit for each student. If table and arm desks are used, make sure left-handed students are not seated at desks designed for right-handers. (kinesthetic)

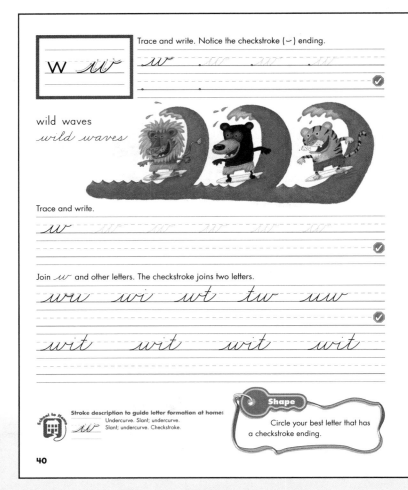

Trace and write. Notice the checkstroke (⌣) ending.

wild waves
wild waves

Trace and write.

Join *w* and other letters. The checkstroke joins two letters.

wu   wi   wt   tw   uw

wit   wit   wit   wit

Stroke description to guide letter formation at home:
Undercurve. Slant; undercurve.
Slant; undercurve. Checkstroke.

Shape
Circle your best letter that has a checkstroke ending.

40

---

1 Present the Letter

Help students focus on the letter **w** by asking:

- How is **w** like **u**? *(Both begin with an undercurve, have slant strokes, three undercurves.)*
- How does **w** end? *(with a checkstroke)*

Model Write **w** on guidelines as you say the stroke description. Model writing **w** in the air as you repeat the stroke description. Have students say the description as they write **w** in the air with you.

Corrective Strategy

Deepen the retrace in the checkstroke before swinging into the undercurve of the next letter.

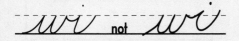 **not**

2 Write and Evaluate

After students have practiced writing **w** on scrap paper or practice boards, ask them to trace and write the first row of letters.

 Stop and Check To help students evaluate **w**, ask:

- Are your slant strokes pulled down straight to the baseline?
- Does your checkstroke begin and end at the midline?

School to Home

Families may use the stroke description on the student page to encourage good letter formation at home. **Practice Master 84** provides take-home practice for the letters **u** and **w**.

3 Apply

Ask students to complete the page by writing **w** and joining it to other letters. Remind students to think about shape as they write, remembering the basic strokes.

PRACTICE MASTER 24

  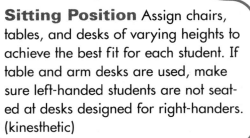

Trace and write.

e *e* *e*

exercise classes
exercise classes

Trace and write.

e

Join *e* and other letters.

ew eu ei et te ie

tie we tweet wet

Shape
Circle your best letter that has an undercurve beginning.

School to Home
Stroke description to guide letter formation at home:
e Undercurve; loop back; slant; undercurve.

41

- Undercurve, loop back, slant, undercurve

Coaching Hint

Extra Practice Keep a record of the letters with which students are having problems. Give students writing exercises such as word lists and tongue twisters that will give them practice with these letters. (visual, kinesthetic)

1. Present the Letter

Help students focus on the letter **e** by asking:
- How does **e** begin? *(with an undercurve)*
- What size letter is **e**? *(short)*

Model Write **e** on guidelines as you say the stroke description. Model writing **e** in the air as you repeat the stroke description. Have students say the words as they use their index finger to write **e** on their desktop.

Corrective Strategy
Be sure there is a loop in the letter.

e   not   *e*

2. Write and Evaluate

After students have practiced writing **e** on scrap paper or practice boards, ask them to trace and write the first row of letters.

 Stop and Check To help students evaluate **e**, ask:
- Does your **e** have a good loop?
- Does your **e** end at the midline?

School to Home

Families may use the stroke description on the student page to encourage good letter formation at home. **Practice Master 85** provides take-home practice for the letters **e** and **l**.

3. Apply

Before the students write, review the basic strokes they have learned. Have them name a letter and tell what strokes are used to make it. Then ask students to complete the page by writing **e** and joining it to other letters, remembering the importance of proper shape.

PRACTICE MASTER 25

T41

• Undercurve, loop back, slant, undercurve

Trace and write. Close the loop at the midline.

lots of little bubbles
lots of little bubbles

Trace and write.

Join *l* and other letters.

li le lt il el wl

lit let tell will

Shape
Circle your best letter that has an undercurve ending.

42

Coaching Hint

Using the Chalkboard

Continue to use the chalkboard for practicing basic strokes, letters, and numerals. Students who have difficulty with motor skills may benefit from the space the chalkboard provides. Since erasing is easy, finding and correcting errors becomes simple. (kinesthetic, visual)

1 Present the Letter

Help students focus on the letter **l** by asking:
• Where does the loop close? *(near the midline)*
• How does **l** end? *(with an undercurve)*

Model Write **l** on guidelines as you say the stroke description. Model writing **l** in the air as you repeat the stroke description. Have students say the words as they take turns writing a large **l** on the chalkboard.

Corrective Strategy

Close the loop just below the midline.

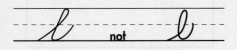

2 Write and Evaluate

After students have practiced writing **l** on scrap paper or practice boards, ask them to trace and write the first row of letters.

 Stop and Check To help students evaluate **l**, ask:
• Does your **l** touch the headline?
• Does your last undercurve touch the midline?

3 Apply

Ask students to complete the page by writing **l** and joining it to other letters. Remind students to think about shape as they write, remembering to check the models frequently.

PRACTICE MASTER 26

School to Home

Families may use the stroke description on the student page to encourage good letter formation at home. **Practice Master 85** provides take-home practice for the letters **e** and **l**.

T42

Trace and write.

b

a banana ballet
a banana ballet

Trace and write.

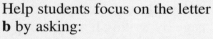

Join *b* and other letters. Notice the checkstroke to undercurve joining.

be bi bl bu ib eb

bell bill tube web

Stroke description to guide letter formation at home:
b Undercurve; loop back; slant; undercurve. Checkstroke.

Shape
Circle your best letter that has a checkstroke ending.

43

- Undercurve, loop back, slant, undercurve
- Checkstroke

Coaching Hint

Basic Strokes Provide sheets of newsprint and a dark crayon for each student. Let students tape their papers to a board or wall and practice the strokes in large, sweeping motions. Have them practice each stroke several times to feel the motion that each one involves. (kinesthetic, visual)

1. Present the Letter

Help students focus on the letter **b** by asking:

- Where does the loop close in **b**? *(near the midline)*
- How does **b** differ from **l**? *(The letter b ends with a check-stroke.)*

Model Write **b** on guidelines as you say the stroke description. Model writing **b** in the air as you repeat the stroke description. Have students say the description as they write **b** in the air with you.

Corrective Strategy

Deepen the checkstroke a bit before swinging into the next letter.

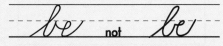
be   not   be

2. Write and Evaluate

After students have practiced writing **b** on scrap paper or practice boards, ask them to trace and write the first row of letters.

Stop and Check To help students evaluate **b**, ask:

- Does your loop close near the midline?
- Does your checkstroke end at the midline?

School to Home

Families may use the stroke description on the student page to encourage good letter formation at home. **Practice Master 86** provides take-home practice for the letters **b** and **h**.

3. Apply

Ask students to complete the page by writing **b** and joining it to other letters. Remind students to consider shape as they write, checking that their letters are easy to read.

PRACTICE MASTER 27

Name:

Trace the letter. Make sure the paper is in the correct position.

b   b   b

b   b   b

Write the letter.
b b b b b b b

Write the letter and the joinings.
b b b b b b b

bu bi bb lb ub eb

Copyright © Zaner-Bloser, Inc.   Practice Master 27

T43

- Undercurve, loop back, slant
- Overcurve, slant, undercurve

Coaching Hint

Positions for Writing Check for correct paper and pencil positions and good posture. When students are writing, call out "freeze." While they are frozen, students should check their writing positions and make necessary adjustments before they "thaw" and begin to write again. (visual, auditory, kinesthetic)

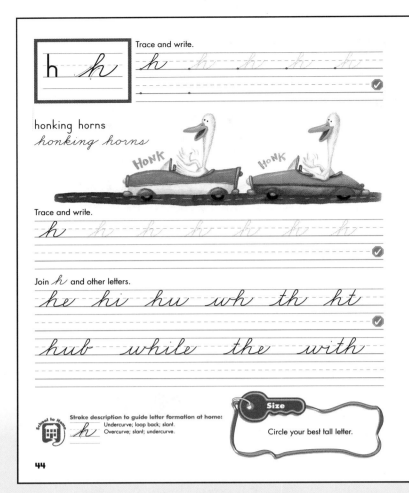

Trace and write.

h h

honking horns
honking horns

Trace and write.

Join *h* and other letters.

he hi hu wh th ht

hub while the with

Stroke description to guide letter formation at home:
h Undercurve; loop back; slant.
Overcurve; slant; undercurve.

Size
Circle your best tall letter.

44

---

1 Present the Letter

Help students focus on the letter **h** by asking:
- What stroke follows the first slant? *(overcurve)*
- How does **h** end? *(with an undercurve)*

Model Write **h** on guidelines as you say the stroke description. Model writing **h** in the air as you repeat the stroke description. Have students say the words as they use their index finger to write **h** in a layer of shaving cream on their desktop.

Corrective Strategy
Close the loop near the midline and keep slant strokes parallel.

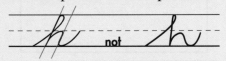

h **not** *h*

T44

2 Write and Evaluate

After students have practiced writing **h** on scrap paper or practice boards, ask them to trace and write the first row of letters.

 Stop and Check To help students evaluate **h,** ask:
- Does your loop close near the midline?
- Does your overcurve touch the midline?

Families may use the stroke description on the student page to encourage good letter formation at home. **Practice Master 86** provides take-home practice for the letters **b** and **h**.

3 Apply

Ask students to complete the page by writing **h** and joining it to other letters. Remind students to use the guidelines to help them form their letters with correct size.

PRACTICE MASTER 28

Name:

Trace the letter. Make sure the paper is in the correct position.

h h h

h h h

Write the letter.

h h h h h h h

Write the letter and the joinings.

h h h h h h h

hi he hu ht th wh

Practice Master 28   Copyright © Zaner-Bloser, Inc.

Trace and write. Notice that the lower loop closes at the baseline.

f

funny footprints
funny footprints

Trace and write.

Join *f* and other letters.

ft   fi   fe   ft   ife

full   beef   fit   left

School to Home
Stroke description to guide letter formation at home:
Undercurve; loop back; slant;
loop forward. Undercurve.

Size
Circle your best letter that has a descender.

45

- Undercurve, loop back, slant, loop forward
- Undercurve

Coaching Hint

Pencil Position Students having difficulty with the conventional method of holding the writing instrument may wish to try the alternate method. (kinesthetic)

---

1. Present the Letter

Help students focus on the letter **f** by asking:
- How does **f** begin and end? *(with an undercurve)*
- Where does the upper loop close? *(near the midline)*

Model Write **f** on guidelines as you say the stroke description. Model writing **f** in the air as you repeat the stroke description. Have students say the words as they use their index finger to write **f** on their desktop.

Corrective Strategy

Close the lower loop near the baseline.

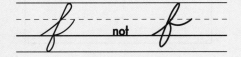

2. Write and Evaluate

After students have practiced writing **f** on scrap paper or practice boards, ask them to trace and write the first row of letters.

 Stop and Check To help students evaluate **f,** ask:
- Does your upper loop close near the midline?
- Does your lower loop close at the baseline?

School to Home

Families may use the stroke description on the student page to encourage good letter formation at home. **Practice Master 87** provides take-home practice for the letters **f** and **k**.

3. Apply

Before they write, ask students to share what they remember about how **f** fits on the guidelines. Ask them to complete the page by writing **f** and joining it to other letters, remembering to make their letters the correct size.

PRACTICE MASTER 29

- Undercurve, loop back, slant
- Overcurve, curve forward, curve under
- Slant right, undercurve

Coaching Hint

Size of Letters Prepare a set of lowercase cursive alphabet cards. Have a student or group of students sort the letters by size. Remind students that **j, p, g, q, y,** and **z** are short letters with descenders that go below the baseline. (visual, kinesthetic)

Trace and write.

k   k   *k*   *k*   *k*   *k*   *k*   *k*

kittens knitting mittens
kittens knitting mittens

Trace and write.

k   k   k   k   k   k   k

Join *k* and other letters.

ke   ki   kl   ike   eek

kit   bike   week   kite

Stroke description to guide letter formation at home:
k Undercurve; loop back; slant.
Overcurve; curve forward;
curve under. Slant right; undercurve.

Size
Circle your best tall letter.

46

---

1 Present the Letter

Help students focus on the letter **k** by asking:
- How does **k** begin and end? *(with an undercurve)*
- How many pauses are in **k**? *(two)*

Model Write **k** on guidelines as you say the stroke description. Model writing **k** in the air as you repeat the stroke description. Have students say the words as they take turns using their index finger to write large **k**'s on the chalkboard, using guidelines that are far apart.

Corrective Strategy

The curve under is followed by a pause, slant right, and undercurve.

k   not   *k*

2 Write and Evaluate

After students have practiced writing **k** on scrap paper or practice boards, ask them to trace and write the first row of letters.

Stop and Check To help students evaluate **k,** ask:
- Does your **k** begin and end with an undercurve?
- Does your upper loop close near the midline?

School to Home

Families may use the stroke description on the student page to encourage good letter formation at home. **Practice Master 87** provides take-home practice for the letters **f** and **k**.

3 Apply

Ask students to complete the page by writing **k** and joining it to other letters. Remind students to check the size of their letters by comparing them with the models.

PRACTICE MASTER 30

Name:

Write the letter.
k   k   k   k   k   k
k   k   k   k   k   k

Write the joinings.
ke   ek   ki   ku   lk   ik

Write the words.
keel   bike   kettle
kit   kite   bulk
like   hike   week

Practice Master 30   Copyright © Zaner-Bloser, Inc.

Trace and write.

r r

a rainbow ride
a rainbow ride

Trace and write.

Join r and other letters.

rl ru ir tr wr ire

rule reel write true

Size
Circle your best short letter.

47

- Undercurve
- Slant right
- Slant, undercurve

Coaching Hint

Hands-On Writing Use the overhead projector to project a letter onto the chalkboard. Ask students to wet their index finger in a cup of water and trace over the letter on the chalkboard as you say the stroke description. (visual, auditory, kinesthetic)

---

1 Present the Letter

Help students focus on the letter **r** by asking:
- What stroke follows the first undercurve? *(slant right)*
- How does **r** end? *(with an undercurve)*

Model Write **r** on guidelines as you say the stroke description. Model writing **r** in the air as you repeat the stroke description. Have students say the description as they write **r** in the air with you.

Corrective Strategy
Pause after the first undercurve and then slant right.

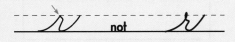

2 Write and Evaluate

After students have practiced writing **r** on scrap paper or practice boards, ask them to trace and write the first row of letters.

Stop and Check To help students evaluate **r**, ask:
- Is your **r** about the same width as the model?
- Are your lines smooth and even?

School to Home

Families may use the stroke description on the student page to encourage good letter formation at home. **Practice Master 88** provides take-home practice for the letters **r** and **s**.

3 Apply

Before students write, call attention to the stroke formation of a particular letter. Remind them that it is important to make each letter the correct size. Ask students to complete the page by writing **r** and joining it to other letters.

PRACTICE MASTER 31

Name:

Write the letter.

Write the joinings.

Write the words.

ruler   rib   rebel
wire   blur   brew
reef   twirl   free

Copyright © Zaner-Bloser, Inc.   Practice Master 31

T47

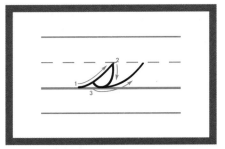

- Undercurve
- Retrace, curve down and back
- Undercurve

Coaching Hint

Letter Practice Draw writing lines on one side of 9-in. × 12-in. pieces of oak tag and laminate one for each student. Students can use these as "slates," practicing their handwriting with a wipe-off crayon or marker. (visual, kinesthetic)

Trace and write.

s   _s_

a slippery surprise
a slippery surprise

Trace and write.

_s_

Join _s_ and other letters.

_se   sk   sl   sw   ss   st_

sweet   skis   bus   wrist

Stroke description to guide letter formation at home:
_s_   Undercurve. Retrace; curve down and back. Undercurve.

Size
Circle your best short letter.

48

---

1 Present the Letter

Help students focus on the letter **s** by asking:

- How is **s** like **r**? *(Both begin and end with an undercurve.)*
- How many retraces are in **s**? *(two)*

Model Write **s** on guidelines as you say the stroke description. Model writing **s** in the air as you repeat the stroke description. Have students say the words as they dip their finger in water and write large **s**'s on the chalkboard.

Corrective Strategy

Be sure the final undercurve rests on the baseline.

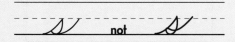
_s_   not   _s_

2 Write and Evaluate

After students have practiced writing **s** on scrap paper or practice boards, ask them to trace and write the first row of letters.

 Stop and Check To help students evaluate **s,** ask:

- Is the bottom of your **s** closed?
- Does your **s** end at the midline?

School to Home

Families may use the stroke description on the student page to encourage good letter formation at home. **Practice Master 88** provides take-home practice for the letters **r** and **s**.

3 Apply

Ask students to complete the page by writing **s** and joining it to other letters. Remind students to think about size as they write, remembering that tall letters touch the headline and short letters touch the midline.

PRACTICE MASTER 32

Name: ___

Write the letter.
_s_   _s s s s s_
_s s s s s_

Write the joinings.
_st si sw ts ls us_

Write the words.
skirt   suit   shirt
still   self   shelf
west   bells   burst

Practice Master 32   Copyright © Zaner-Bloser, Inc.

Trace and write. Notice the overcurve ending.

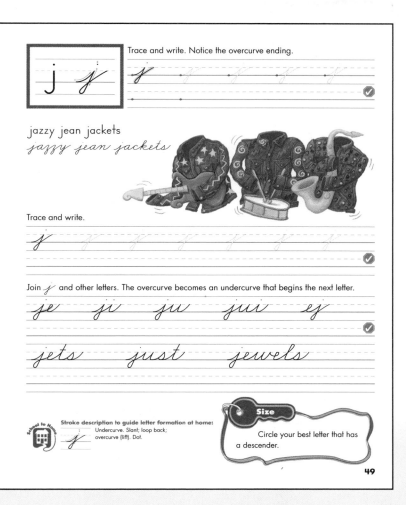

jazzy jean jackets
jazzy jean jackets

Trace and write.

Join *j* and other letters. The overcurve becomes an undercurve that begins the next letter.

je   ji   ju   jui   ej

jets   just   jewels

Stroke description to guide letter formation at home:
Undercurve. Slant; loop back;
overcurve (lift). Dot.

Size
Circle your best letter that has a descender.

49

- Undercurve
- Slant, loop back, overcurve, (lift)
- Dot

1. Present the Letter

Help students focus on the letter **j** by asking:
- Where does **j** begin? (*at the baseline*)
- Where does the overcurve end? (*near the midline*)

Model Write **j** on guidelines as you say the stroke description. Model writing **j** in the air as you repeat the stroke description. Have students say the description as they use their index finger to write **j** on their desktop.

Corrective Strategy
Make sure the overcurve ending stops at the baseline to blend with the undercurve beginning.

ju not *jc*

2. Write and Evaluate

After students have practiced writing **j** on scrap paper or practice boards, ask them to trace and write the first row of letters.

Stop and Check To help students evaluate **j,** ask:
- Is your slant stroke pulled through the baseline?
- Does your loop close near the baseline?

3. Apply

Ask students to complete the page by writing **j** and joining it to other letters. Remind students to think about size as they write, remembering to compare their letters with the models frequently.

PRACTICE MASTER 33

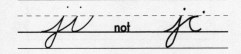

- Undercurve
- Slant, loop back, over-curve, curve back
- Undercurve

Trace and write.

p p p p p p p

pajama party
pajama party

Trace and write.

p p p p p p p p

Join *p* and other letters.

pi pe pl pr ph sp

put push beep spell

Stroke description to guide letter formation at home:
Undercurve. Slant; loop back; overcurve; curve back. Undercurve.

Size
Circle your best letter that has a descender.

50

---

1. Present the Letter

Help students focus on the letter **p** by asking:

- Where does the beginning undercurve end? *(at the midline)*
- Where does the loop close? *(near the baseline)*

Model Write **p** on guidelines as you say the stroke description. Model writing **p** in the air as you repeat the stroke description. Have students say the description as they write **p** in the air with you.

Corrective Strategy

End with a retraced undercurve.

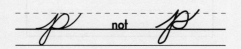

p not *p*

2. Write and Evaluate

After students have practiced writing **p** on scrap paper or practice boards, ask them to trace and write the first row of letters.

Stop and Check To help students evaluate **p,** ask:

- Does your loop fill the descender space?
- Does your loop slant to the left?

3. Apply

Ask students to complete the page by writing **p** and joining it to other letters. Remind them to write their letters with consistent and correct size.

PRACTICE MASTER 34

T50

Practice

i   t   u   w

e   l   b   h   f   k

r   s   j   p

Write these rhyming words.

keep   peep   jeep

jet   pet   set   wet

hill   bill   fill   will

true   blue   flew

51

Review the Letters

Direct the students to look at the letters being reviewed on student page 51. Ask them what they remember about the shape of these letters. (*All begin with an undercurve.*)

Review the stroke descriptions and model again any of the letters the students may be having difficulty writing.

Ask a volunteer to give a verbal description of one of these letters: **i, t, u, w, e, l, b, h, f, k, r, s, j, p**. Challenge the other students to identify the letter being described and then write it on guidelines on the chalkboard.

Write and Evaluate

Have the students write the rhyming words on student page 51, remembering to form letters with correct shape and size.

✓ **Stop and Check** To help students evaluate their writing, ask:

- Did you write with correct strokes so your letters have good shape?
- Did you use the guidelines to make letters with correct size?
- Do your short letters touch both the midline and the baseline?
- Do your tall letters touch both the headline and the baseline?
- Do your short letters with descenders touch the headline of the next writing space?

Corrective Strategy

When **w** is the initial letter, emphasize the checkstroke to undercurve joining.

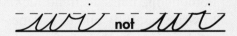 *wi* **not** *wi*

More About Practice

Because handwriting is a motor skill that becomes automatic over time, practice makes permanent, not necessarily perfect. Asking students to write letters and words many times without stopping to evaluate can reinforce bad habits and lead to sloppy, rushed work. Instead, have students write several letters and words and then check their writing for one or more of the Keys to Legibility.

Application

Application

Homophones Homophones are words that sound alike but are spelled differently. They have different meanings, too. Look at these examples.

| see sea | hour our | knew new | deer dear |

Write these homophone pairs.

fur fir *be bee*

peer pier *flew flu*

its it's *wheel we'll*

their there *sweet suite*

blue blew

Keys to Legibility

My writing has good shape. ☐
My writing has good size. ☐

52

Apply

Read the directions on student page 52 with the students and review the example homophones. Then have the students write the homophone pairs. Remind them to write carefully and to use the guidelines to help them form letters with proper shape and correct size.

Help students summarize what they have learned about shape and size. Then have them respond to the checklist in the Key feature.

Special Helps
Maureen King
Occupational Therapist

To develop the arches of the hand and refine the student's ability to hold and use writing implements, try this activity. Provide a round laundry cup. Have the student use his or her thumb and fingertips to rotate, or slowly spin, the cup on a table surface. Fill the cup halfway with water to increase feedback.

As the student becomes more adept in carrying out the activity, have him or her do the same motion—but using the thumb and fingertips to turn the cup in the air, palm facing up. Replace the cup with a smaller disk-shaped object such as a checker game piece.

Coaching Hint
Left-Handed Writers

Right-handed teachers can invite a left-handed person to serve as a handwriting model for left-handed students. Another teacher, an older student, or a parent could visit the classroom to assist left-handed writers. Make sure the model demonstrates correct pencil and paper positions for the left-handed writer. (visual)

Write Downcurve Letters

a

You will learn to write these lowercase letters. Each letter begins with a downcurve stroke.

a   d   g   o   c   q

Trace and write downcurve strokes.

Keys to Legibility

Make your writing easy to read. As you write downcurve letters, you will pay attention to the spacing of your writing.

Spacing

There should be space for ○ between letters.

betdteens

There should be space for \ between words.

between words

53

Featured Letters

a   d   g

o   c   q

Featured Key to Legibility:

Spacing

Students will consider **spacing** as they evaluate their writing.

Other Acceptable Letterforms

These are acceptable variations of the models in this book.

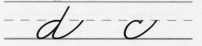

d   c

---

1. Present the Letters

Point out the lowercase letters on the page, and explain that each one begins with a downcurve stroke. Encourage students to use their finger or a pencil to trace several of the downcurve strokes in these letters. Then have them trace and write the downcurve strokes on the guidelines.

Direct the students to notice the stop-and-check logo at the end of the writing grid. Remind them that this symbol tells them to stop and check their writing. Guide the students in circling their best downcurve stroke on each line.

2. Present the Key

Point out the Key feature on the student page. Explain to students that they will see this feature often in the lessons that follow. This Key helps them consider the spacing in their writing as they evaluate legibility.

What the research says . . .

The mental processes involved in handwriting . . . are connected to other important learning functions, such as storing information in memory, retrieving information, manipulating letters, and linking them to sound when spelling.
—Cheryl Murfin Bond, "Handwriting Instruction: Key to Good Writing," *Seattle's Child & Eastside Parent*

Teaching the Letters:
Modeling

Modeling is a *think aloud* process in which a teacher verbalizes his or her thinking while working through a particular strategy. The stroke descriptions aid the modeling process. For example, in modeling the letter **a,** the teacher might say, "As I write the letter **a,** I know I start near the broken midline. Then I curve down and under, back up to the midline. Now am I finished? No, I have to slant down and then finish with an undercurve to the midline."

- Downcurve, undercurve
- Slant, undercurve

Coaching Hint

Spacing As students continue the transition from manuscript to cursive, they may find that maintaining correct spacing between letters is difficult. The joining stroke between letters must be wide enough to allow for good spacing. There should be just enough space for a small oval. (visual, kinesthetic)

Trace and write. Notice the downcurve beginning.

a   a   a   a   a   a   a

alphabet quackers
alphabet quackers

Trace and write.

a   a   a   a   a   a   a   a

Join *a* and other letters. Notice the undercurve to downcurve joining.

aa   ea   ra   al   aw   as

treat   all   awhile   ask

Stroke description to guide letter formation at home:
a Downcurve; undercurve.
Slant; undercurve.

Spacing
Circle your best joining.

54

---

1 Present the Letter

Help students focus on the letter **a** by asking:
- Where does the downcurve stroke begin? *(just below the midline)*
- How much of **i** do you see in **a**? *(all except the dot)*

Model Write **a** on guidelines as you say the stroke description. Model writing **a** in the air as you repeat the stroke description. Have students say the words as they use their index finger to write large **a**'s on sandpaper.

Corrective Strategy

The undercurve to downcurve joining becomes a doublecurve.

ac **not** *au*

2 Write and Evaluate

After students have practiced writing **a** on scrap paper or practice boards, ask them to trace and write the first row of letters.

✔ **Stop and Check** To help students evaluate **a**, ask:
- Is your **a** closed?
- Does your **a** end at the midline?

Families may use the stroke description on the student page to encourage good letter formation at home. **Practice Master 90** provides take-home practice for the letters **a** and **d**.

3 Apply

Ask students to complete the page by writing **a** and joining it to other letters. Remind students to think about spacing as they write, remembering to leave more space between words than between letters within a word.

PRACTICE MASTER 35

Trace and write.

d d *d d d d d d* ✓

a daisy duet
a daisy duet

Trace and write.

d d d d d d d d ✓

Join *d* and other letters.

da de di dd ad ide ✓

dessert added wide

 Stroke description to guide letter formation at home:
d Downcurve; undercurve.
Slant; undercurve.

Spacing
Circle your best joining.

55

- Downcurve, undercurve
- Slant, undercurve

Coaching Hint

Left-Handed Writers Encourage students to hold their hands and wrists correctly. Using good pencil and paper position will help left-handed writers succeed in handwriting. (kinesthetic)

1 Present the Letter

Help students focus on the letter **d** by asking:
- Where does **d** begin? (*just below the midline*)
- Can you see **a** in **d**? (*yes*)

Model Write **d** on guidelines as you say the stroke description. Model writing **d** in the air as you repeat the stroke description. Have students say the words as they write **d** in the air with you.

Corrective Strategy

Pull the slant stroke toward the baseline with a good retrace.

d not *d*

2 Write and Evaluate

After students have practiced writing **d** on scrap paper or practice boards, ask them to trace and write the first row of letters.

✓ **Stop and Check** To help students evaluate **d,** ask:
- Does your downcurve meet with the undercurve at the midline?
- Does your **d** end at the midline?

School to Home

Families may use the stroke description on the student page to encourage good letter formation at home. **Practice Master 90** provides take-home practice for the letters **a** and **d**.

3 Apply

Ask students to complete the page by writing **d** and joining it to other letters. Remind students to think about spacing as they write, following the spacing in the models.

PRACTICE MASTER 36

Name:

Write the letter.

d d d d d
d d d d d

Write the joinings.
da id ad dd ld ud

Write the words.
deed date dusk
desk dish dial
add head build

Practice Master 36   Copyright © Zaner-Bloser, Inc.

- Downcurve, undercurve
- Slant, loop back, overcurve

Coaching Hint

Practice Joinings Have students form letters and joinings in a thin layer of finger paint spread on aluminum foil. (kinesthetic)

Trace and write. Notice the overcurve ending.

g g

a soggy, shaggy dog
a soggy, shaggy dog

Trace and write.

g

Join g and other letters. Notice the overcurve to downcurve joining.

ga   gg   gi   gh   gr   gl

gift   grade   wiggle

School to Home Stroke description to guide letter formation at home:
g Downcurve; undercurve.
Slant; loop back; overcurve.

Spacing Circle a word you wrote that has good joinings.

56

1. Present the Letter

Help students focus on the letter **g** by asking:

- What stroke follows the slant? *(loop back)*
- Where does the loop in **g** close? *(near the baseline)*

Model Write **g** on guidelines as you say the stroke description. Model writing **g** in the air as you repeat the stroke description. Have students say the description as they use their index finger to write **g** on their desktop.

Corrective Strategy

The overcurve ends at the beginning of the downcurve.

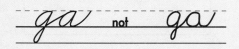
ga not *ga*

2. Write and Evaluate

After students have practiced writing **g** on scrap paper or practice boards, ask them to trace and write the first row of letters.

Stop and Check To help students evaluate **g,** ask:

- Is your letter closed at the top?
- Does your loop close near the baseline?

School to Home

Families may use the stroke description on the student page to encourage good letter formation at home. **Practice Master 91** provides take-home practice for the letters **g** and **o**.

3. Apply

Ask students to complete the page by writing **g** and joining it to other letters. Remind students to think about spacing as they write, remembering that the joinings between letters determine the spacing in cursive words.

PRACTICE MASTER 37

T56

Trace and write.

Trace and write.

poodles eating noodles
poodles eating noodles

Join *o* and other letters. Notice the checkstroke to downcurve joining.

od oa oo ot or oll

other orders boat

Stroke description to guide letter formation at home:
o Downcurve; undercurve. Checkstroke.

Spacing
Circle your best joining.

- Downcurve, undercurve
- Checkstroke

Coaching Hint

Sitting Position Correct body position allows students to write without tiring. Encourage students to sit comfortably erect with their feet flat on the floor and their hips touching the back of the chair. Both arms rest on the desk. (kinesthetic)

---

1 Present the Letter

Help students focus on the letter **o** by asking:
- Where does **o** begin? (*just below the midline*)
- Where does **o** end? (*at the midline*)

Model Write **o** on guidelines as you say the stroke description. Model writing **o** in the air as you repeat the stroke description. Have students say the description as they use their index finger to write **o** on their desktop.

Corrective Strategy
The checkstroke swings wide to join a downcurve.

oa not oa

2 Write and Evaluate

After students have practiced writing **o** on scrap paper or practice boards, ask them to trace and write the first row of letters.

✔ **Stop and Check** To help students evaluate **o,** ask:
- Is your oval closed?
- Does your checkstroke end at the midline?

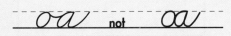

School to Home

Families may use the stroke description on the student page to encourage good letter formation at home. **Practice Master 91** provides take-home practice for the letters **g** and **o**.

3 Apply

Ask students to complete the page by writing **o** and joining it to other letters. Remind students to form their checkstrokes correctly so their **o**'s will join easily to the next letter and provide correct spacing.

PRACTICE MASTER 38

• Downcurve, undercurve

Coaching Hint

Hands-On Writing Provide a shallow tray or box lid with a thin layer of sand in it. Allow students to form letters and joinings in the sand while they say the stroke descriptions. (auditory, kinesthetic)

Trace and write.

c c

ice cream accident
ice cream accident

Trace and write.

Join c and other letters.

ce cl cr ice uce

called cried could

 School to Home Stroke description to guide letter formation at home:
Downcurve; undercurve.

Spacing Circle a word you wrote that has good joinings.

58

---

1. Present the Letter

Help students focus on the letter **c** by asking:
• Where does **c** begin? *(below the midline)*
• How does **c** end? *(with an undercurve)*

Model Write **c** on guidelines as you say the stroke description. Model writing **c** in the air as you repeat the stroke description. Have students say the words as they use their index finger to write large **c**'s on their desktop.

Corrective Strategy

Swing wide on the undercurve to undercurve joining.

ci   not   ci

2. Write and Evaluate

After students have practiced writing **c** on scrap paper or practice boards, ask them to trace and write the first row of letters.

✓ **Stop and Check** To help students evaluate **c**, ask:
• Does your **c** have correct slant?
• Does your **c** end at the midline?

 School to Home

Families may use the stroke description on the student page to encourage good letter formation at home. **Practice Master 92** provides take-home practice for the letters **c** and **q**.

3. Apply

Ask students to complete the page by writing **c** and joining it to other letters. Remind students to think about spacing as they write, keeping their letters and words spaced like the models.

PRACTICE MASTER 39

T58

Trace and write.

a quick quarterback
a quick quarterback

Trace and write.

Join *q* and other letters.

qu   quo   qua   qui   que

quite   quarter   quote

Spacing

Circle your best joining.

59

- Downcurve, undercurve
- Slant, loop forward
- Undercurve

Coaching Hint

Joinings To stress correct joining strokes, ask a volunteer to write a word in cursive on the chalkboard. Then have a second volunteer use colored chalk to highlight the joining strokes. (visual)

1 Present the Letter

Help students focus on the letter **q** by asking:
- How does **q** begin? *(with a downcurve)*
- Where does the loop in **q** close? *(near the baseline)*

Model Write **q** on guidelines as you say the stroke description. Model writing **q** in the air as you repeat the stroke description. Have students say the description as they write **q** in the air with you.

Corrective Strategy
Close the loop near the baseline.

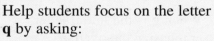

2 Write and Evaluate

After students have practiced writing **q** on scrap paper or practice boards, ask them to trace and write the first row of letters.

Stop and Check: To help students evaluate **q,** ask:
- Does your loop close near the baseline?
- Does your loop fill the descender space?

School to Home

Families may use the stroke description on the student page to encourage good letter formation at home. **Practice Master 92** provides take-home practice for the letters **c** and **q.**

3 Apply

Ask students to complete the page by writing **q** and joining it to other letters. Remind students to think about spacing as they write, remembering to leave the correct amount of space between letters and between words.

PRACTICE MASTER 40

T59

Practice

a d g o c q

Write the names of breakfast foods.

quiche   cereal   eggs

toast   bagel   bread

Write the phrases.

a quart of grape juice

a good breakfast

Review the Letters

Direct the students to look at the letters being reviewed on student page 60. Ask them what they remember about the shape of these letters. (*All begin with a downcurve.*)

Review the stroke descriptions and model again any of the letters the students may be having difficulty writing.

Ask a volunteer to give a verbal description of one of these letters: **a, d, g, o, c, q**. Challenge the other students to identify the letter being described and then write it on guidelines on the chalkboard.

Write and Evaluate

Have the students write the words for breakfast foods on student page 60, remembering to form letters and words with correct shape, size, and spacing.

 Stop and Check To help students evaluate their writing, ask:

- Did you write with correct strokes so your letters have good shape?
- Did you use the guidelines to make letters with correct size?
- Do your short letters touch both the midline and the baseline?
- Do your tall letters touch both the headline and the baseline?
- Do your short letters with descenders touch the headline of the next writing space?
- Did you use good spacing between letters and words?

Corrective Strategy

When **g** is the initial letter, emphasize the overcurve to undercurve joining.

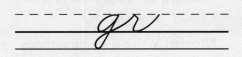

More About Practice

Handwriting practice is most beneficial when it is done in the student's primary modality. Auditory learners can take turns saying stroke descriptions for each other to write. Visual learners might use colored chalk to highlight specific strokes in a letter. Kinesthetic learners will enjoy using their finger to trace letters on a tactile surface, such as sandpaper.

Application

Nouns Nouns are naming words. These nouns name vegetables.

Write the words.

peas carrots peppers

lettuce cabbages leeks

potatoes squash broccoli

Complete the sentences.

I like _____ .

I don't like _____ .

Keys to Legibility

My writing has good shape. ☐
My writing has good size. ☐
My writing has good spacing. ☐

61

Apply

Read the explanation of nouns on student page 61 with the students and review the examples. Then have the students write the names of the vegetables. Remind them to write carefully and to use the guidelines to help them form letters with proper shape, correct size, and good spacing.

Help students summarize what they have learned about shape, size, and spacing. Then have them respond to the checklist in the Key feature.

Special Helps
Maureen King
Occupational Therapist

Students who have difficulty writing on a horizontal surface may benefit from extra practice at the chalkboard. Writing on a vertical surface allows the wrist to remain in a more normal and more efficient position, and the writing then strengthens and reinforces correct wrist and hand position.

When students are writing on worksheets, allow a few students to secure the sheets to the chalkboard with magnets or tape and complete their work on the vertical surface. As students gain control, gradually reduce the number of magnets. You may wish to make this a permanent rotating workstation in your classroom.

Coaching Hint

Pencil Position Errors in line quality may be a result of holding the pencil too tightly, using the fingers to draw the stroke, forming the stroke too quickly, varying the pressure on the pencil, or tilting the pencil at different angles. (kinesthetic)

- Slant

- Slant
- Curve forward, slant
- Curve right

- Slant
- Curve forward and back
- Curve forward and back

- Slant
- Slide right, (lift)
- Slant

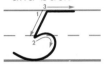

- Slant
- Curve forward and back, (lift)
- Slide right

- Curve down and forward, loop

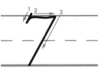

- Slant
- Doublecurve
- Slant

- Curve back and down, curve back, slant up

- Downcurve, undercurve
- Slant

- Slant, (lift)
- Downcurve, undercurve

T62

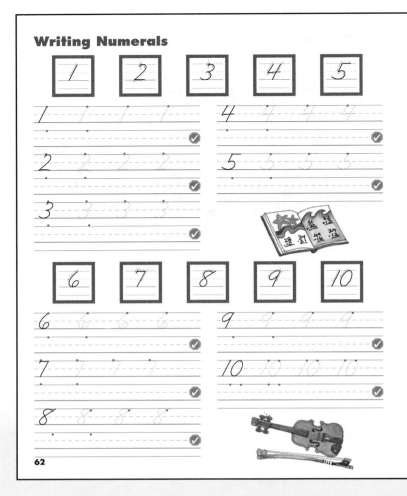

Writing Numerals

62

Present the Numerals

Help students focus on the numeral **1** by asking:

- Where does **1** begin? *(at the headline)*
- How many strokes are in **1**? *(one)*

Model Write **1** on guidelines as you say the stroke description. Model writing **1** in the air as you repeat the stroke description. Have students say it as they write **1** in the air with you.

Corrective Strategy

All cursive numerals are tall.

Write and Evaluate

After students have practiced writing **1** on scrap paper or practice boards, ask them to trace and write the first row of numerals.

 Stop and Check To help students evaluate **1,** ask:

- Does your **1** begin at the headline?
- Does your **1** have correct slant?

Repeat teaching steps 1 and 2 for the numerals 2–10.

To help students evaluate **2–10,** ask:

- Does your **2** begin with a short slant stroke?
- Are the top and bottom of your **3** about the same size?
- Is the slide right of your **4** on the midline?

SAM'S BUSY DAY

9:00	Reading
10:30	Math
11:30	Social Studies
12:30	Lunch
1:15	Gym
2:00	Science
3:00	School's Out
4:00	Homework
5:00	Violin Lesson
6:00	Dinner
7:00	Free Time
9:00	Sleep

1. When does Sam start his homework? _____

2. When does Sam eat lunch? _____

3. When does Sam have math? _____

4. When does Sam go home? _____

5. When does Sam go to sleep? _____

6. When does Sam have his violin lesson? _____

63

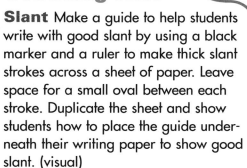

Coaching Hint

Slant Make a guide to help students write with good slant by using a black marker and a ruler to make thick slant strokes across a sheet of paper. Leave space for a small oval between each stroke. Duplicate the sheet and show students how to place the guide underneath their writing paper to show good slant. (visual)

- Does your **5** touch both the headline and the baseline?
- Does the loop of your **6** end at the baseline?
- Does the top of your **7** have a slight doublecurve?
- Does your **8** begin just below the headline?
- Is your **9** written with correct slant?
- Is there correct space between the **1** and **0** in your **10**?

3 Apply

Direct students' attention to the chart on student page 63 about Sam's busy day. Point out and explain the use of the colon in writing times. Then ask students to complete the page by writing the appropriate times to answer the questions. Remind them that cursive numerals are written with consistent forward slant.

Corrective Strategy
The numerals should rest on the baseline.

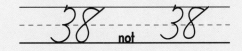

PRACTICE MASTERS 73–74

Numerals

1 2 3 4 5 6 7 8 9 10

Write the numerals.

1 1 1	4 4 4 4
2 2 2	5 5 5 5
3 3 3 3	
6 6 6	9 9 9 9
7 7 7	10 10 10 10
8 8 8 8	

Copyright © Zaner-Bloser, Inc.   Practice Master 73

Practice Master 74   Copyright © Zaner-Bloser, Inc.

Manuscript Maintenance

Manuscript Maintenance

Read this postcard. The writer made his letters small enough to fit the space on the postcard.

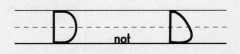

message

Dear Paul,
    I am in Washington, D.C.
We're at the National Air
and Space Museum. I wish
you were here.
            Brian

Paul Parker   address
22 Baker Street
Chicago, IL 60657

Write Brian's postcard, or write one of your own. Use manuscript writing.
Remember to write a message and a mailing address.
Make your writing fit the space.

64

1. Review Manuscript

Direct the students to look at the postcard on student page 64. Ask them to describe what they remember about the shape, size, spacing, and slant of letters, words, and numerals written in manuscript.

Review the stroke descriptions and model again any of the letters or numerals the students may be having difficulty writing. Refer them to the Cursive and Manuscript alphabets on student pages 22 and 23 for more guidance.

Ask students to notice how the writer of the postcard adjusted the size of the writing to fit the smaller space. Point out that shape, size, spacing, and slant remain consistent even though the writing is smaller than usual.

2. Write and Evaluate

Have the students write a postcard message and a mailing address on student page 64, remembering to form the letters and numerals carefully so they will be legible.

Stop and Check To help students evaluate their writing, ask:
- Did you write with correct strokes so your letters and numerals have good shape?
- Did you write letters and numerals with good size to fit the writing space?
- Did you allow good spacing?
- Did you maintain good vertical slant?

Corrective Strategy

The slide right and slide left strokes are the same width.

not

T64

Write Overcurve Letters

You will learn to write these lowercase letters. Each letter begins with an overcurve stroke.

n   m   y   x   v   z

Trace and write overcurve strokes.

Keys to Legibility

Make your writing easy to read. As you write overcurve letters, you will pay attention to the slant of your writing.

Slant

Remember that cursive letters have a consistent forward slant.

even slant

To write with good slant:

POSITION • Check your paper position.
PULL • Pull your downstrokes in the proper direction.
SHIFT • Shift your paper as you write.

65

Featured Key to Legibility:

Slant

Students will consider **slant** as they evaluate their handwriting.

Other Acceptable Letterforms

These are acceptable variations of the models in this book.

---

1. Present the Letters

Point out the lowercase letters on the page, and explain that each one begins with an overcurve stroke. Encourage students to use their finger or a pencil to trace several of the overcurve strokes in these letters. Then have them trace and write the overcurve strokes on the guidelines.

Direct the students to notice the stop-and-check logo at the end of the writing grid. Remind them that this symbol tells them to stop and check their writing. Guide the students in circling their best overcurve stroke.

2. Present the Key

Point out the Key feature on the student page. This Key helps them consider the slant of their writing as they evaluate legibility.

What the research says ...

When we teach and value handwriting, we are sending a message to students and parents that we value legibility, attention to detail, neatness, correctness, and excellence.
—Reggie Routman, "We Still Need to Teach and Value Handwriting," *Literacy at the Crossroads: Crucial Talk About Reading, Writing, and Other Teaching Dilemmas*

Teaching the Letters:
Warming Up for Writing

Motivate students for writing by having them do some warm-up writing first. The warm-up activity may be having them write undercurve and slant strokes to draw a line of waves on their papers. Demonstrate drawing the waves on the chalkboard as you repeat the strokes aloud: "Undercurve, slant, undercurve, slant." Warming up this way will help students begin a piece of writing with success and confidence.

- Overcurve, slant
- Overcurve, slant, undercurve

Coaching Hint

Evaluating Slant Write the word *minimum* on the chalkboard in cursive and in manuscript. Use parallel lines of colored chalk to highlight the difference between manuscript verticality and cursive slant. (visual)

Trace and write. Notice the overcurve beginning.

n *n*

a wonderful picnic
a wonderful picnic

Trace and write.

Join *n* and other letters. Notice the undercurve to overcurve joining.

nn sn kn na nd ne

knight   band   inn

School to Home
Stroke description to guide letter formation at home:
n   Overcurve; slant.
       Overcurve; slant; undercurve.

Slant
Circle a letter you wrote that has good slant.

66

---

1 Present the Letter

Help students focus on the letter **n** by asking:

- What stroke follows the first slant? *(overcurve)*
- How many overcurves are in **n**? *(two)*

Model Write **n** on guidelines as you say the stroke description. Model writing **n** in the air as you repeat the stroke description. Have students say the words as they use their index finger to write large **n**'s on their desktop.

Corrective Strategy

The undercurve to overcurve joining becomes a doublecurve with no retrace.

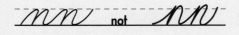

nn not *nn*

2 Write and Evaluate

After students have practiced writing **n** on scrap paper or practice boards, ask them to trace and write the first row of letters.

 Stop and Check To help students evaluate **n,** ask:

- Do your overcurves touch the midline?
- Are the tops of your **n** round?

School to Home

Families may use the stroke description on the student page to encourage good letter formation at home. **Practice Master 93** provides take-home practice for the letters **n** and **m**.

3 Apply

Ask students to complete the page by writing **n** and joining it to other letters. Remind students that correct slant is determined by correct paper position and the direction of the downstrokes.

PRACTICE MASTER 41

Name:

Write the letter.
n   n   n   n   n
n   n   n   n   n   n

Write the joinings.
ni   nt   nk   gn   on   no

Write the words.
nation   narrow   nice
canal   town   dance
corn   cent   notice

Copyright © Zaner-Bloser, Inc.   Practice Master 41

Trace and write.

m _m_

_m   m   m   m_

mysterious masks
mysterious masks

Trace and write.

_m   m   m   m   m   m_

Join _m_ and other letters.

me   mo   ma   ime   ame

month   slammed   might

Slant
Circle a word you wrote that has good slant.

67

_m_

- Overcurve, slant
- Overcurve, slant
- Overcurve, slant, undercurve

Coaching Hint

Left-Handed Writers The Zaner-Bloser *Writing Frame* can help students achieve correct hand position because the hand holding the pencil and resting over the frame automatically settles into the correct position. (kinesthetic)

---

1 Present the Letter

Help students focus on the letter **m** by asking:

- How many slant strokes are in **m**? *(three)*
- How many times does **m** touch the midline? *(four)*

Model Write **m** on guidelines as you say the stroke description. Model writing **m** in the air as you repeat the stroke description. Have students say the words as they dip their index finger in water and write large **m**'s on the chalkboard.

Corrective Strategy

Be careful when joining **m** to the next letter.

_mm_ **not** _mm_

2 Write and Evaluate

After students have practiced writing **m** on scrap paper or practice boards, ask them to trace and write the first row of letters.

 Stop and Check To help students evaluate **m,** ask:

- Is there enough space between your overcurves?
- Are your slant strokes parallel?

School to Home

Families may use the stroke description on the student page to encourage good letter formation at home. **Practice Master 93** provides take-home practice for the letters **n** and **m**.

3 Apply

Ask students to complete the page by writing **m** and joining it to other letters. Remind students to think about slant as they write, remembering to pull their slant strokes toward the baseline before they begin the next stroke.

PRACTICE MASTER 42

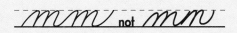

- Overcurve, slant, undercurve
- Slant, loop back, overcurve

Coaching Hint

Joinings Keep a record of joinings students are having problems with. Provide practice with these joinings by assigning writing exercises such as making word lists and writing tongue twisters. Call students' attention to less common joinings when they occur in daily writing assignments. (visual, auditory, kinesthetic)

Trace and write.

eyes spying
eyes spying

Trace and write.

Join *y* and other letters. Notice the overcurve to overcurve joining.

ym   yn   ye   ty   cy

yellow   your   city   gym

Stroke description to guide letter formation at home:
Overcurve; slant; undercurve.
Slant; loop back; overcurve.

Slant
Circle a letter you wrote that has good slant.

68

---

1 Present the Letter   ## 2 Write and Evaluate   ## 3 Apply

1 Present the Letter

Help students focus on the letter **y** by asking:
- How does **y** end? *(with an overcurve)*
- How many overcurves are in **y**? *(two)*

Model Write **y** on guidelines as you say the stroke description. Model writing **y** in the air as you repeat the stroke description. Have students say the description as they write **y** in the air with you.

Corrective Strategy
The overcurve ending crosses the slant stroke at the baseline.

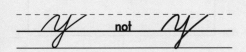

2 Write and Evaluate

After students have practiced writing **y** on scrap paper or practice boards, ask them to trace and write the first row of letters.

✓ **Stop and Check** To help students evaluate **y,** ask:
- Does your loop close at the baseline?
- If you turn your paper upside down, does your **y** look like an **h**?

School to Home

Families may use the stroke description on the student page to encourage good letter formation at home. **Practice Master 94** provides take-home practice for the letters **y** and **x**.

3 Apply

Ask students to complete the page by writing **y** and joining it to other letters. Remind students to think about slant as they write, checking that their slant lines are parallel.

PRACTICE MASTER 43

Name:
Write the letter.
Write the joinings.
Write the words.

Copyright © Zaner-Bloser, Inc.   Practice Master 43

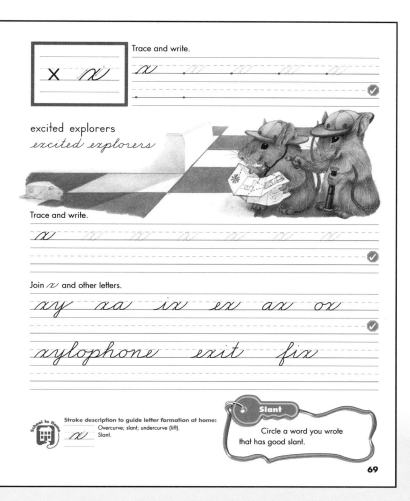

x 𝓍 | Trace and write.

excited explorers
excited explorers

Trace and write.

Join 𝓍 and other letters.

xy xa ix ex ax ox

xylophone exit fix

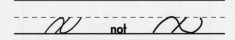
School to Home
Stroke description to guide letter formation at home:
Overcurve; slant; undercurve (lift).
Slant.

Slant
Circle a word you wrote that has good slant.

69

- Overcurve, slant, undercurve, (lift)
- Slant

Coaching Hint

Evaluation Write a few words and sentences with several obvious errors on the chalkboard. Have volunteers come to the chalkboard to locate, identify, and correct the errors. (visual, kinesthetic)

1 Present the Letter

Help students focus on the letter **x** by asking:
- Where does the overcurve end? *(at the midline)*
- Where does the last slant stroke end? *(at the baseline)*

Model Write **x** on guidelines as you say the stroke description. Model writing **x** in the air as you repeat the stroke description. Have students say the words as they dip their index finger in water and write **x** on the chalkboard.

Corrective Strategy

After writing the overcurve, be sure the slant stroke is pulled toward the baseline.

𝓍 **not** 𝓍

2 Write and Evaluate

After students have practiced writing **x** on scrap paper or practice boards, ask them to trace and write the first row of letters.

✓ **Stop and Check** To help students evaluate **x,** ask:
- Does your **x** have a good overcurve?
- Is your **x** crossed near the middle of the first slant stroke?

School to Home

Families may use the stroke description on the student page to encourage good letter formation at home. **Practice Master 94** provides take-home practice for the letters **y** and **x**.

3 Apply

Ask students to complete the page by writing **x** and joining it to other letters. Remind students to think about slant as they write, remembering to compare their letters with the models.

PRACTICE MASTER 44

Name:
Write the letter.
𝓍 𝓍 𝓍 𝓍 𝓍 𝓍
𝓍 𝓍 𝓍 𝓍 𝓍 𝓍
Write the joinings.
xu xu xa ix ix ax
Write the words.
taxi ox axis
wax tax six
tuxedo mixer waxy

Practice Master 44   Copyright © Zaner-Bloser, Inc.

T69

- Overcurve, slant, undercurve
- Checkstroke

Coaching Hint

Correct Slant

Most errors in slant can be corrected in one of the following ways:
1. Check paper position.
2. Pull the slant strokes in the proper direction.
3. Shift the paper as the writing progresses across the line.

Trace and write.

five volleyballs on vacation
five volleyballs on vacation

Trace and write.

Join *v* and other letters. Notice the checkstroke to overcurve joining.

vy vi va ove ive ave

envy very visitor

Stroke description to guide letter formation at home:
Overcurve; slant; undercurve.
Checkstroke.

Slant
Circle a letter you wrote that has good slant.

---

1 Present the Letter

Help students focus on the letter **v** by asking:
- What strokes are in **v**? *(overcurve, slant, undercurve, checkstroke)*
- How does **v** end? *(with a checkstroke)*

Model Write **v** on guidelines as you say the stroke description. Model writing **v** in the air as you repeat the stroke description. Have students say the words as they use their index finger to write large **v**'s on their desktop.

Corrective Strategy

Join the checkstroke correctly to the downcurve of the next letter.

vo not *vo*

2 Write and Evaluate

After students have practiced writing **v** on scrap paper or practice boards, ask them to trace and write the first row of letters.

 Stop and Check To help students evaluate **v,** ask:
- Does your **v** have a good overcurve beginning?
- Does your **v** end with a checkstroke?

Families may use the stroke description on the student page to encourage good letter formation at home. **Practice Master 95** provides take-home practice for the letters **v** and **z**.

3 Apply

Ask students to complete the page by writing **v** and joining it to other letters. Remind students to think about slant as they write, remembering to write letters with consistent forward slant.

PRACTICE MASTER 45

Name:

Write the letter.

Write the joinings.
vi va vu vo ov vy

Write the words.
voice vent voyage
velvet vowel viper
flavor heavy hive

Copyright © Zaner-Bloser, Inc.   Practice Master 45

Trace and write.

z z 𝓏 𝓏 𝓏 𝓏 𝓏 𝓏 ✓

amazing mazes
amazing mazes

Trace and write.

𝓏 𝓏 𝓏 𝓏 𝓏 𝓏 𝓏 𝓏 ✓

Join 𝓏 and other letters.

zy zi ze za ize oze ✓

zebra zipper zigzag

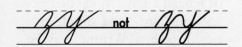 Stroke description to guide letter formation at home:
Overcurve; slant. Overcurve;
curve down; loop; overcurve.

 Slant
Circle a word you wrote
that has good slant.

71

- Overcurve, slant
- Overcurve, curve down,
  loop, overcurve

 Coaching Hint

Using the Chalkboard Place cups of water near the chalkboard. Invite students to practice writing strokes, letters, joinings, and words you call out by dipping their fingers or paintbrushes into the water and writing on the board. (auditory, kinesthetic)

1. Present the Letter

Help students focus on the letter **z** by asking:
- What stroke follows the first slant? *(overcurve)*
- How does **z** end? *(with an overcurve)*

Model Write **z** on guidelines as you say the stroke description. Model writing **z** in the air as you repeat the stroke description. Have students say the description as they write **z** in the air with you.

Corrective Strategy
Help students make the overcurve to overcurve joining correctly.

 not

2. Write and Evaluate

After students have practiced writing **z** on scrap paper or practice boards, ask them to trace and write the first row of letters.

✓ **Stop and Check** To help students evaluate **z,** ask:
- Does your loop close near the baseline?
- Does your loop fill the descender space?

 School to Home

Families may use the stroke description on the student page to encourage good letter formation at home. **Practice Master 95** provides take-home practice for the letters **v** and **z.**

3. Apply

Ask students to complete the page by writing **z** and joining it to other letters. Remind students to think about slant as they write, remembering that correct slant makes their writing easy to read.

PRACTICE MASTER 46

Name:

Write the letter.
𝓏 𝓏 𝓏 𝓏 𝓏 𝓏
𝓏 𝓏 𝓏 𝓏 𝓏 𝓏

Write the joinings.
ze zo zi za zu zy

Write the words.
snooze frozen haze
crazy freeze size
jazz razor dizzy

Practice Master 46   Copyright © Zaner-Bloser, Inc.

Practice

$$n \quad m \quad y \quad x \quad v \quad z$$

Write these color words.

maroon   lime   orange

neon green   tangerine

violet   lavender   silver

yellow   ivory   azure

pink   a color mix

Complete this sentence.

My favorite color is _____.

72

Review the Letters

Direct the students to look at the letters being reviewed on student page 72. Ask them what they remember about the shape of these letters. (*All begin with an overcurve.*)

Review the stroke descriptions and model again any of the letters the students may be having difficulty writing.

Ask a volunteer to give a verbal description of one of these letters: **n, m, y, x, v, z**. Challenge the other students to identify the letter being described and then write it on guidelines on the chalkboard.

Write and Evaluate

Have the students write the color words on student page 72, remembering to write with consistent forward slant.

✓ **Stop and Check** To help students evaluate their writing, ask:

- Are your beginning overcurves rounded?
- Do your short letters touch both the midline and the baseline?
- Do your tall letters touch both the headline and the baseline?
- Do your short letters with descenders touch the headline of the next writing space?
- Did you leave correct spacing between the letters in your words?
- Does your writing have good slant?

Corrective Strategy

The undercurve to downcurve joining becomes a double-curve.

More About Practice

The development and maintenance of good handwriting skills depend on meaningful practice. Possible writing activities include friendly letters, jokes and riddles (*Highlights for Children* magazines are good sources for these), nametags or labels, charts, vocabulary or spelling cards, and simple stories or poems. Writing may be done in cooperative groups.

Application

What a great day for a picnic!
Write these phrases that describe the picture.

marvelous gigantic salad

amazing icy lemonade

tasty turkey sandwiches

yummy yellow mustard

juicy melon

Keys to Legibility

My writing has good shape. ☐
My writing has good size. ☐
My writing has good spacing. ☐
My writing has good slant. ☐

excellent pie

73

Apply

Read the directions on student page 73 with the students and review the items shown in the illustration. Then have the students write the describing phrases. Remind them to write carefully with consistent slant and to leave good spacing between letters and words.

Help students summarize what they remember about the Keys to Legibility. Then have them respond to the checklist in the Key feature.

Special Helps
Maureen King
Occupational Therapist

To improve students' coordination and strengthen awareness of crossing the body's midline, provide a vertical game such as Connect Four. Position the game toward the student's left side (for right-handers). As the game is played, challenge students to pick up and move each game piece with the right hand, using the left hand to stabilize the game board. (Reverse for left-handers.)

Coaching Hint

Slant To help students improve slant, draw parallel slant lines and have a student change them into the slant strokes of a word. (visual, kinesthetic)

slant

Review Lowercase Letters

Tell students they now have studied and written all the lowercase cursive letterforms. Guide them in a review of these letters with the following activity.

1. The letters **b, e, f, h, i, j, k, l, p, r, s, t, u,** and **w** begin with the _____ stroke. (*undercurve*)

2. The letters **a, c, d, g, o,** and **q** begin with the _____ stroke. (*downcurve*)

3. The letters that begin with the overcurve stroke are _____. (*m, n, v, x, y, z*)

4. The letters **f, g, j, p, q, y,** and **z** have a _____. (*descender*)

5. The letters **b, o, v,** and **w** end with a _____. (*checkstroke*)

Have students review and practice the basic cursive strokes.

*Use **Practice Masters 16–20** for additional practice with lowercase letters and the Keys to Legibility.*

Review Lowercase Letters

a   b   c   d   e   f   g
n   o   p   q   r   s   t

Write these lowercase letters in cursive.

i t u w

e l b h f

k r s j p

a d g o c q

n m y x v z

Write these words in cursive.

cozy		mixed	
happy		lively	
swift		brave	
great		juicy	
young		quick	

74

Write the Letters

Encourage students to use their best cursive handwriting as they write the lowercase letters and words on student page 74 and rearrange the letters to write new words on student page 75. Remind students to consider the Keys to Legibility as they write.

Evaluate

To help students evaluate their writing, ask questions such as these:
- Which of your letters are satisfactory?
- Which of your letters need improvement?
- Did you use the guidelines to write letters with correct size?
- Did you dot your **i**'s and **j**'s and cross your **t**'s and **x**'s?

h   i   j   k   l   m

u   v   w   x   y   z

Change the order of the letters to write a new word.

deal   pat   late

~~lead~~

ate   trap   pool

tens   dear   limes

nap   ant

won   tone

Keys to Legibility

Shape
Size
Spacing
Slant

My writing has good shape. ☐
My writing has good size. ☐
My writing has good spacing. ☐
My writing has good slant. ☐

75

Coaching Hint

Evaluation Help students realize the importance of good handwriting in all subject areas. The Zaner-Bloser *Handwriting Evaluation Stamp* encourages students to consider the legibility of their handwriting on content-area papers. (visual)

Certificates of Progress *(Practice Master 76) should be awarded to those students who show notable handwriting progress and* **Certificates of Excellence** *(Practice Master 77) to those who progress to the top levels of handwriting ability.*

Application of Legibility Skills

Students at this level should realize the importance of legibility beyond the daily handwriting lesson. Their skills must be transferred into all areas of the curriculum. An awareness of the importance of handwriting legibility in all subjects will encourage the students to maintain the skills learned. When this awareness is developed, students will have formed good handwriting habits that will stay with them throughout their lives.

Remind students that the four Keys to Legibility all begin with the letter **s** (**shape, size, spacing,** and **slant**), making them easy to remember. It is hoped that students will eventually perform evaluations mentally, applying the four keys as a check of the legibility of their writing.

Joinings

Remind students they have studied and written the lowercase cursive letters grouped according to beginning strokes. Write the cursive lowercase alphabet on the chalkboard and guide students in choosing the letters that complete each category of the chart below.

undercurve ending letters (a, c, d, e, f, h, i, k, l, m, n, p, q, r, s, t, u, x)	undercurve beginning letters (i, t, u, w, r, s, p, j, e, l, h, k, f, b)
overcurve ending letters (g, j, y, z)	downcurve beginning letters (a, c, d, q, g, o)
checkstroke ending letters (b, o, v, w)	overcurve beginning letters (n, m, x, y, z, v)

Tell students that joinings are formed by combining any letter from one column with a letter from the other column. If we choose the letter **a** from the left column and write it with the letter **i** from the right column, we have joined an undercurve-ending letter with an undercurve-beginning letter to form the undercurve to undercurve joining **ai**.

Choose several of these joinings and list them on the chalkboard:

**undercurve to undercurve
undercurve to downcurve
undercurve to overcurve
overcurve to undercurve
overcurve to downcurve
overcurve to overcurve
checkstroke to undercurve
checkstroke to downcurve
checkstroke to overcurve**

Have students choose letter pairs to form examples of each joining. List their suggestions on the chalkboard with the proper joining label.

T76

Joinings

Write each joining. Then write the word.

Undercurve to Undercurve

ri   ride   ti   time

Undercurve to Downcurve

ea   eat   mo   moon

Undercurve to Overcurve

ry   cry   az   amaze

76

Write and Evaluate

Direct students to look at the joinings and words on student pages 76 and 77. Ask if any joinings are still difficult for them to write correctly. Discuss why such joinings may be tricky to write.

Have students write the joinings and the words on the student pages. Remind them to consider the Keys to Legibility as they write.

To help students evaluate their writing, ask questions such as these:
• Which of your joinings are satisfactory?
• Which of your joinings need improvement?

Corrective Strategy

Swing wide on the undercurve to undercurve joining.

ai **not** *ai*

Deepen the checkstroke a little before swinging into the undercurve of the next letter.

be **not** *be*

Overcurve to Undercurve

ju   *just*   *ye*   *yell*

Overcurve to Downcurve

ga   *gate*   *yo*   *you*

Overcurve to Overcurve

zy   *dizzy*   *gy*   *foggy*

Checkstroke to Undercurve

wr   *wrote*   *os*   *most*

Checkstroke to Downcurve

ba   *back*   *vo*   *voices*

Checkstroke to Overcurve

om   *home*   *ov*   *over*

77

Coaching Hints

Spacing As students continue the transition from manuscript to cursive, they may find that maintaining correct spacing between cursive letters is difficult. The joining stroke between letters must be wide enough to allow for good spacing. There should be just enough space for a minimum-sized oval. Suggest students practice joinings to reinforce both fluent strokes and good spacing. (visual, kinesthetic)

Using the Chalkboard
Use the chalkboard for teaching and practicing the basic strokes, letters, and joinings. Students having difficulty with fine motor skills may benefit from the increased spacing the chalkboard provides. Since erasing is easy, identifying and correcting errors becomes a simpler task. (visual, auditory, kinesthetic)

Joinings Have the students refer to the list of joinings they worked with in the introductory chart described on page T76. Point out that not all letter combinations will appear in words *(lx, mz, qg, qx)*. Have students try to find examples of each of the letter combinations in words and write the words next to their matching combinations. Have the students circle combinations they cannot find in words. Have them underline combinations they find most often in words *(na, ni, ca, me, da, bo, bi)*.

Encourage students to compare and discuss their answers and draw conclusions about the most common joinings, least common joinings, joinings that do not occur in our language, and the joinings they find most difficult. You may wish to keep track of the joinings that seem to cause the most difficulty and provide frequent practice with these combinations in letter pairs and in words.

Jokes and Riddles Invite students to write jokes or riddles in cursive. Allow students to take turns sharing the jokes or riddles with classmates. Any issue of the *Highlights for Children* magazine will provide several riddles students may use as models.

Literature Connection

Words About Books, pp. 99, 117 Help students understand the terms *title, author,* and *illustrator*. Show a favorite book. Point to the title and say, "This is the title of the book." Read the title aloud. Point to the author's name and say, "This is the name of the author." (Read the name aloud.) "An author is a person who writes a book." Mime writing for students with rudimentary English proficiency. Point to the illustrator's name and say, "This is the name of the illustrator." (Read the name aloud.) "An illustrator is a person who draws or paints the images in a book." Mime drawing or painting as needed. Show a few illustrations in the book.

Writing a Book Review, p. T100 Writing a book review requires students to summarize or retell important parts of a story. Having students retell a story helps to clarify their level of understanding. It is important to differentiate between students' comprehension and their ability to produce language. Allowing students to use picture clues will give you a greater sense of their understanding. Help students write simple sentences to explain what the pictures represent. Students can practice reading the sentences independently. Another option is to allow students to act out the story or use puppets in the retelling.

Vocabulary Development

Calendar Words, pp. T100–T120

Months of the Year You can relate the first languages of some students to English by using cognates—words from other languages that share a common origin, similar pronunciations, and similar meanings with corresponding English words. For example, you can use cognates from Romance languages, such as Spanish, to teach the months of the year (*enero/January, febrero/February, marzo/March, abril/April, mayo/May, junio/June, julio/July, agosto/August, septiembre/September, octubre/October, noviembre/November, diciembre/December*).

Days of the Week Read aloud the names of the days of the week and have students repeat them in chorus. Listen for the correct pronunciation of **th** when students say *Thursday*. Model the correct pronunciation by emphasizing **th** in the first syllable.

Have students create personal calendars to extend their understanding of calendar words. Encourage them to mark important events, holidays, and birthdays. Numbering the months in sequence (January is 1, February is 2, and so on) can help those students from cultures in which months are most often referred to by their position in a sequence.

More About th Many students incorrectly make an s sound when saying words that begin with **th**. (For example, *thought* sounds like *sought*, and *think* sounds like *sink*.) Teach students the correct positioning of the tongue (between the teeth). Ongoing practice and self-corrective techniques will reduce the frequency of this pronunciation problem.

Specific Teaching Tips

Authentic literature exposes students to American culture and teaches elements of language. Use authentic literature to teach those elements that best address students' needs. For example, use a story to emphasize vocabulary and sentence structure. If your focus is on pronunciation and intonation, read the story aloud. You can also read aloud to model conversational strategies.

When choosing a story, determine how much background you need to provide to make it intelligible. Allow students to read the story in their native language first. Reading in a student's first language builds comprehension. Then, when students read the story in English, they can focus on fluency rather than decoding.

Consider using authentic literature from students' native culture.

Fun and Games

Ready, Set, Write! p. T79 When explaining this strategy, discuss what is expected at each stage. First, call students' attention to the word *ready*. Explain that *ready* means "prepared." Explain that *set* means "in position." You might act out the starting stance of a runner in a footrace as you say, "Ready, set, go!" and "On your mark, get set, go!"

Coaching Hint

Teaching Handwriting, p. T109 Students benefit from activities that promote meaningful and natural communication. Have students teach one another how to write cursive forms of specific letters. Reciprocal teaching is appropriate for students at all language levels because it encourages students to express or show their understanding of content both visually and orally. You can also use reciprocal teaching to assess students' fluency and comprehension.

Reciprocal teaching uses several cognitive strategies: visualizing, summarizing, and questioning. Before students begin this exercise, model each strategy. It might be helpful to break down the lesson into small blocks of content for students to present. One way to accomplish this is to group letters formed by making similar strokes.

Visualizing: Explain that visualizing the letters is an important first step in reciprocal teaching. Picturing the letter first will help students guide their partners.

Summarizing: Students will need to recall the steps in a letter's formation and be able to describe each stroke clearly.

Questioning: Students use questioning to help clarify content and to lead their partner in assessing what is right or wrong in his or her work. For example, students in the role of teacher might ask, "Did you use the proper shape? Is the letter the proper size?"

Special Helps

Sequencing and Word Order, p. T109 Students at this level may be both emergent speakers and emergent readers. Help them develop word recognition and improve reading comprehension with activities that require them to order and reorder lines and events from stories, cartoons, and poems. Depending on students' language proficiency, vary the level of difficulty. For example, students with the most limited vocabulary should start with sentences consisting of only three or four words.

To complete the activity on page T109, create cards for each word in the cartoon. Arrange the cards in piles; each pile should contain the words of one line from the cartoon. On the board, write the first line of text from the cartoon. Read the text aloud as you point to each word. Take the word cards for this line and shuffle them. Lay out the cards in random order. Invite a volunteer to place the cards in the proper order and read the line aloud. Repeat this process with the other lines of text.

CULTURAL NOTES

Students may not be familiar with American holidays. Provide background to help them understand their significance. Explain why the occasion or event is remembered. Use pictures to show the origin of a holiday and a typical American celebration of it. Invite students to share holidays or special events celebrated in their home culture. Have them explain the significance of the holiday, and encourage them to share events customary to the occasion.

Writing Uppercase Letters

Keys to Legibility

Remind students that good handwriting is legible handwriting. The most important thing to remember is that readers must be able to read a message in order to understand its meaning.

Brainstorm with students about the qualities of legible handwriting. Write responses on the chalkboard. These might include neatness, carefully written letters, and letters that are not too crowded.

Point out that the four Keys to Legibility are easy to remember because they all start with **s: shape, size, spacing,** and **slant.**

Review that **shape** describes the strokes that form each letter and give it a unique appearance. **Size** describes the height of letters. **Spacing** describes the space between letters, words, and sentences. **Slant** refers to the angle of writing on the paper. Using these Keys will help the students improve the legibility of their uppercase cursive letters.

Use the **Keys to Legibility Wall Chart** *for more information.*

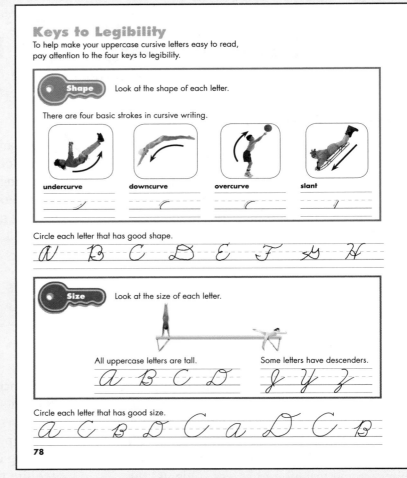

Review Shape and Size

Read and discuss with students the background information and the illustrations on student page 78. Then help them as needed as they complete the activities on the page.

Students having difficulty with correct letter shape may need reinforcement of the basic strokes. Remind students that cursive writing is made up of four basic strokes: undercurve, downcurve, overcurve, slant. Additional practice with these strokes will benefit the student.

Coaching Hints

Hands-On Writing Use the overhead projector to project a letter onto the chalkboard. Ask students to wet their index fingers in a cup of water and trace over the stroke you name. (visual, auditory, kinesthetic)

Using Guidelines Review with students the use of the guidelines for correct letter formation. As you demonstrate on the chalkboard, have students do the following on practice paper:

• Draw over the baseline with a red crayon or marker.

• Draw over the headline and midline with a blue crayon or marker.

(kinesthetic, visual, auditory)

Ready, Set, Write! This strategy will help students use correct positions when they write. Explain that before students write, they should say "Ready," "Set," and "Write" quietly to themselves, following certain directions after each word.

I. Ready: Position the chair in front of the desk or table, leaving enough room to sit comfortably and lean forward from the hips. Keep feet flat on the floor and place arms on the desktop.

2. Set: Position the paper properly on the desk or table and hold the pencil in the correct position.

3. Write: Begin writing.

Help students practice the strategy by calling out "Ready, Set, Write" and asking students to follow the steps. Encourage them to use the strategy on their own whenever they write.

Review Spacing and Slant

Read and discuss with students the background information and the illustrations on student page 79. Help them as needed as they complete the activities on the page.

Tell students that in cursive writing, correct spacing is key to legible handwriting. The beginning stroke of one word should start near the ending stroke of the preceding word. A slanted line drawn from the end point of the last stroke to the baseline should touch both words. There should be room for an uppercase **O** between sentences.

Show an example of cursive writing with correct spacing on the chalkboard. Use colored chalk to draw slanted lines.

Remind students that in cursive writing, all letters should have uniform forward slant.

Coaching Hints

Slant Practicing slant lines at the chalkboard is a good way to improve poor slant strokes. Have students use soft, oversized chalk, holding it as they would hold a pencil. You may want to begin by placing sets of two dots about six inches apart and at the correct slant to mark the starting and stopping points of each slant stroke. (kinesthetic, visual)

Spacing Allow left-handed students to write at the chalkboard, where they can practice keeping their hands below the line of writing. (kinesthetic, visual)

Featured Letters

Featured Key to Legibility:

Students will consider **shape** as they evaluate their writing.

Other Acceptable Letterforms

These are acceptable variations of the models in this book.

Teaching the Letters:
Meaningful Practice

The teacher can use handwriting practice to build self-esteem in students. For example, students can copy a sentence from the chalkboard that contains letters or joinings to practice. On the reverse side, students should practice writing the sentence several times, using the chalkboard model as a guide. Finally, students should turn the paper over and write the sentence again, under their first attempt. Often when students see improvement in their handwriting, they feel better about themselves and are encouraged to strive for further improvement.

Write Downcurve Letters

You will learn to write these uppercase letters. Each letter has a downcurve stroke.

A   O   D   C   E

Trace and write downcurve strokes.

Keys to Legibility

Make your writing easy to read. As you write downcurve letters, you will pay attention to the shape of your writing.

Remember the four basic strokes in cursive writing.

undercurve   downcurve   overcurve   slant

---

1 Present the Letters

Point out the uppercase letters on the page, and explain that each one begins with a downcurve stroke. Encourage students to use their finger or a pencil to trace several of the downcurve strokes in these letters. Then have them trace and write the downcurve strokes on the guidelines.

Direct the students to notice the stop-and-check symbol at the end of the writing grid. Remind them that this symbol tells them to stop and check their writing. Then guide the students in circling their best downcurve stroke.

2 Present the Key

Point out the Key feature on the student page. Explain to students that they will see this feature often. The Keys help them consider certain qualities of good writing as they evaluate their work.

What the research says...

While the content of a student's written effort is admittedly more important than its appearance, some degree of proficiency in the mechanical aspects of writing is needed to prevent interruption in the flow of communicative intent.
—Lisa A. Kurtz, "Helpful Handwriting Hints," *Teaching Exceptional Children*, Vol. 27

Trace and write.

A a a a a a a

Alita arrives in Alaska.
Alita arrives in Alaska.

Trace and write.

a a a a a a a

a is joined to the letter that follows. Write words that begin with *a*.

America August April

Write the sentence.

Alita is amazed.

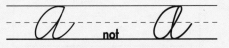
Stroke description to guide letter formation at home:
a Downcurve; undercurve.
Slant; undercurve.

 Shape
Circle your best letter that has a downcurve beginning.

81

- Downcurve, undercurve
- Slant, undercurve

Coaching Hint

Teaching Handwriting Write each student's name on a self-adhesive ruled name strip. Laminate it if you wish. Place the name strip on the student's desk to serve as a permanent model. (kinesthetic, visual)

---

1. Present the Letter

Help students focus on the letter **A** by asking:
- How many strokes are in **A**? *(four)*
- How does **A** end? *(with an undercurve)*

Model Write **A** on guidelines as you say the stroke description. Model writing **A** in the air as you repeat the stroke description. Have students say the description as they write **A** in the air with you.

Corrective Strategy
Pause before writing the slant stroke.

a not *a*

2. Write and Evaluate

After students have practiced writing **A** on scrap paper or practice boards, ask them to trace and write the first row of letters.

 Stop and Check To help students evaluate **A,** ask:
- Is your **A** closed?
- Do you have a good slant stroke?

 School to Home

Families may use the stroke description on the student page to encourage good letter formation at home. **Practice Master 96** provides take-home practice for the letters **A** and **O**.

3. Apply

Ask students to complete the page by writing **A** and the words and sentence. Remind students to think about shape as they write, remembering to sit in good writing position and to form their letters carefully.

PRACTICE MASTER 47

Name:
a Write the letter and the words.
a a a a a
a a a a a a
Akron Amazon Aruba
Alena Amos Archie
Write the sentences.
Alice is in Alaska
Avery was in Alabama
Copyright © Zaner-Bloser, Inc.   Practice Master 47

T81

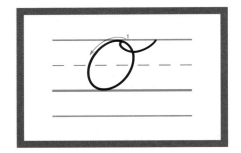

- Downcurve, undercurve, loop, curve right

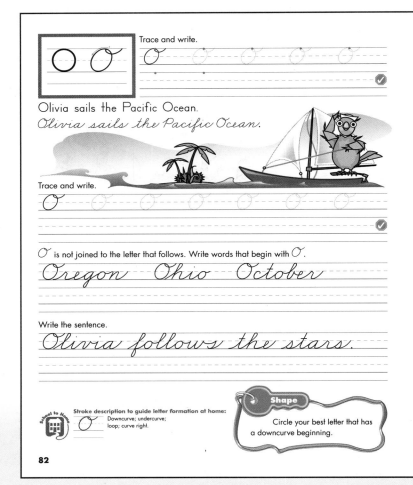

Trace and write.

$\mathcal{O}$ $\mathcal{O}$ ✓

Olivia sails the Pacific Ocean.
Olivia sails the Pacific Ocean.

Trace and write.

$\mathcal{O}$ ✓

$\mathcal{O}$ is not joined to the letter that follows. Write words that begin with $\mathcal{O}$.

Oregon   Ohio   October

Write the sentence.

Olivia follows the stars.

School to Home Stroke description to guide letter formation at home:
$\mathcal{O}$ Downcurve; undercurve; loop; curve right.

Shape Circle your best letter that has a downcurve beginning.

82

Coaching Hint

Left-Handed Writers At the chalkboard, left-handed writers should stand in front of the writing lines and pull the downstrokes to the left elbow. The elbow is bent, and the writing is done at a comfortable height. Step to the right often to maintain correct slant. (visual, kinesthetic)

1 Present the Letter

Help students focus on the letter **O** by asking:
- Where does **O** begin? *(just below the headline)*
- How many pauses are in **O**? *(none)*

Model Write **O** on guidelines as you say the stroke description. Model writing **O** in the air as you repeat the stroke description. Have students say the description as they use paintbrushes dipped in water to write large **O**'s on the chalkboard.

Corrective Strategy
Dip the loop down slightly, then curve right to end at the headline.

$\mathcal{O}$ not $\mathcal{O}$

2 Write and Evaluate

After students have practiced writing **O** on scrap paper or practice boards, ask them to trace and write the first row of letters.

✓ **Stop and Check** To help students evaluate **O**, ask:
- Does your **O** begin below the headline?
- Does your **O** end near the headline?

School to Home

Families may use the stroke description on the student page to encourage good letter formation at home. **Practice Master 96** provides take-home practice for the letters **A** and **O**.

3 Apply

Ask students to complete the page by writing **O** and the words and sentence. Remind students to think about shape as they write, remembering to compare their writing with the models.

PRACTICE MASTER 48

Name:

Write the letter and the words.

$\mathcal{O}$ $\mathcal{O}$ $\mathcal{O}$ $\mathcal{O}$ $\mathcal{O}$ $\mathcal{O}$
$\mathcal{O}$ $\mathcal{O}$ $\mathcal{O}$ $\mathcal{O}$ $\mathcal{O}$ $\mathcal{O}$

Oakland   Oz   Oxford
Oswald   Onyx   Ozzie

Write the sentences.
Oscar drove to Ottawa

Owen is going to Oregon

Practice Master 48   Copyright © Zaner-Bloser, Inc.

T82

Student Page (83)

Trace and write.

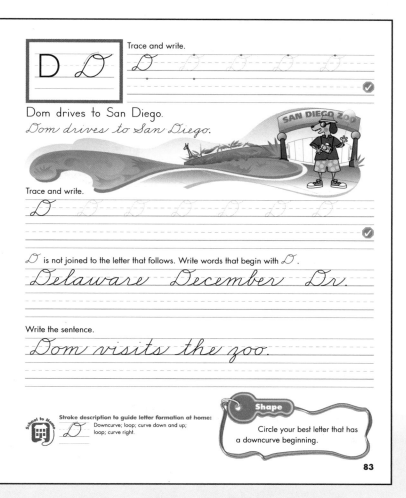

D D D D D D D

Dom drives to San Diego.
Dom drives to San Diego.

Trace and write.

D D D D D D D

D is not joined to the letter that follows. Write words that begin with D.

Delaware December Dr.

Write the sentence.

Dom visits the zoo.

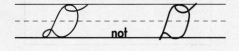

Stroke description to guide letter formation at home:
D Downcurve; loop; curve down and up; loop; curve right.

Shape
Circle your best letter that has a downcurve beginning.

83

- Downcurve, loop, curve down and up, loop, curve right

---

1 Present the Letter

Help students focus on the letter **D** by asking:
- How many loops are in **D**? *(two)*
- How many times does **D** touch the baseline? *(two)*

Model Write **D** on guidelines as you say the stroke description. Model writing **D** in the air as you repeat the stroke description. Have students say the description as they use their index finger to trace the model in their book.

Corrective Strategy
The first loop of **D** is open and rests on the baseline.

D not D

2 Write and Evaluate

After students have practiced writing **D** on scrap paper or practice boards, ask them to trace and write the first row of letters.

Stop and Check To help students evaluate **D**, ask:
- Is your **D** closed?
- Does your **D** end near the headline?

School to Home

Families may use the stroke description on the student page to encourage good letter formation at home. **Practice Master 97** provides take-home practice for the letters **D** and **C**.

3 Apply

Ask students to complete the page by writing **D** and the words and sentence. Remind students to think about shape as they write, remembering that correct shape is dependent on correctly written strokes.

PRACTICE MASTER 49

- Slant
- Downcurve, undercurve

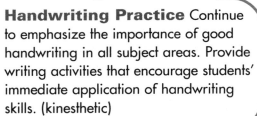

Coaching Hint

Handwriting Practice Continue to emphasize the importance of good handwriting in all subject areas. Provide writing activities that encourage students' immediate application of handwriting skills. (kinesthetic)

Trace and write.

Cara comes to California.
Cara comes to California.

Trace and write.

𝒞 is joined to the letter that follows. Write words that begin with 𝒞.

California Colorado Casey

Write the sentence.

Crests are fun to ride.

School to Home — Stroke description to guide letter formation at home:
𝒞 Slant. Downcurve; undercurve.

Shape Circle your best letter that has an undercurve ending.

84

---

1 Present the Letter

Help students focus on the letter **C** by asking:

- How does **C** begin? *(with a slant)*
- What follows the slant? *(down-curve)*

Model Write **C** on guidelines as you say the stroke description. Model writing **C** in the air as you repeat the stroke description. Have students say the description as they write **C** in the air with you.

Corrective Strategy

A short slant begins at the headline.

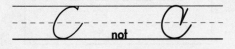

2 Write and Evaluate

After students have practiced writing **C** on scrap paper or prac-tice boards, ask them to trace and write the first row of letters.

Stop and Check To help students evaluate **C,** ask:

- Does your **C** have correct slant?
- Does your **C** end at the mid-line?

School to Home

Families may use the stroke description on the student page to encourage good letter formation at home. **Practice Master 97** provides take-home practice for the letters **D** and **C.**

3 Apply

Ask students to complete the page by writing **C** and the words and sentence. Remind them to write their letters with consistent and correct shape.

PRACTICE MASTER 50

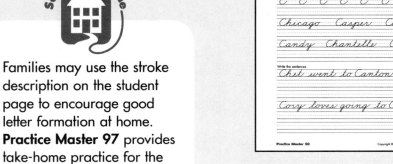

Trace and write.

Esteban floats to England.
Esteban floats to England.

Trace and write.

𝓔 is joined to the letter that follows. Write words that begin with 𝓔.

England   English   Earth

Write the sentence.

Everyone is excited.

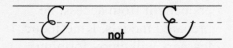 Stroke description to guide letter formation at home:
𝓔 Slant. Downcurve; loop; downcurve; undercurve.

 Shape
Circle your best letter that has an undercurve ending.

85

- Slant
- Downcurve, loop, downcurve, undercurve

1 Present the Letter

Help students focus on the letter **E** by asking:
- How many loops are in **E**? *(one)*
- Where does **E** end? *(at the midline)*

Model Write **E** on guidelines as you say the stroke description. Model writing **E** in the air as you repeat the stroke description. Have students say the words as they use their index finger to write large **E**'s on their desktop.

Corrective Strategy

The bottom downcurve is larger and farther to the left.

𝓔 not 𝓔

2 Write and Evaluate

After students have practiced writing **E** on scrap paper or practice boards, ask them to trace and write the first row of letters.

✓ **Stop and Check** To help students evaluate **E,** ask:
- Is your loop at the midline?
- Are your downcurves the correct size?

 School to Home

Families may use the stroke description on the student page to encourage good letter formation at home. **Practice Master 98** provides take-home practice for the letters **E** and **N**.

3 Apply

Ask students to complete the page by writing **E** and the words and sentence. Remind students to think about shape as they write, remembering to compare their letters with the models.

PRACTICE MASTER 51

Name:

Write the letter and the words.
𝓔 𝓔 𝓔 𝓔 𝓔 𝓔
𝓔 𝓔 𝓔 𝓔 𝓔 𝓔
Egypt   Essex   Elida
Enid   Ebony   Elijah
Write the sentences.
Etta flew to Ethiopia
Emma drove to Elmhurst

Copyright © Zaner-Bloser, Inc.   Practice Master 51

Practice

Practice

a O D C E

Write names for a guest list.

Chris Chu   David Allen

Olivia Ames   Alex Olmos

Chip Dodd   Ellen Avila

Craig Estes   Emilia Cruz

Write the names of your classmates that begin with these letters.

Review the Letters

Direct the students to look at the letters being reviewed on student page 86. Ask them what they remember about the shape of these letters. (*All begin with a downcurve or a short slant followed by a downcurve.*)

Review the stroke descriptions and model again any of the letters the students may be having difficulty writing.

Ask a volunteer to give a verbal description of one of these letters: **A, O, D, C, E**. Challenge the other students to identify the letter being described and then write it on guidelines on the chalkboard.

Write and Evaluate

Have the students write the names on the page, remembering to form their letters with correct strokes so they will have proper shape.

 Stop and Check To help students evaluate their writing, ask:

- Did you write with correct strokes so your letters would have good shape?
- Are your letters about the same width as the models?
- Is your **A** closed?
- Does your **O** end near the head-line?
- Is the loop in your **E** at the midline?

Corrective Strategy

O and **D** do not connect to the following letter.

Ot Dr

More About Practice

Handwriting practice is most beneficial when done in the student's strongest learning modality. Students can take turns saying stroke descriptions so auditory learners can write what they hear. Visual learners benefit from accessible prepared models. Kinesthetic learners will enjoy forming letters with ropes of clay.

T86

Application
Writing an Invitation

Come One, Come All!
Celebrate Arbor Day

At: Chris Edson's house
Address: 5 Ocean Avenue

Date: April 29
Don't bring any treats.

Write the invitation.

Keys to Legibility
My writing has good *shape*. ☐

87

Apply

Read the text of the invitation on student page 87, and review the *What?, Where?,* and *When?* information. Then have the students write the invitation, remembering to form their letters with correctly written strokes so they will have good shape.

Shape

Help students summarize what they have learned about shape. Then have them respond to the item in the Key feature.

Special Helps
Maureen King
Occupational Therapist

Students who have difficulty using the eraser on their pencil efficiently will benefit from this activity. Write ten small circles on a piece of writing paper. Have the student color in the first circle, rotate the pencil by turning it with the thumb and fingertips of the writing hand so the eraser is pointing down, and erase the second circle and so on.

For maximum benefit from this activity, watch students to make sure they are not pressing the pencil down on the desktop for assistance in turning the pencil. Challenge students to refine distal control by using only two fingers and the thumb to rotate the pencil.

Coaching Hint
Using the Chalkboard
The chalkboard permits easy integration of handwriting instruction with other content areas and with day-to-day communication in your classroom. When you have written words or sentences on the board, invite volunteers to trace your writing with colored chalk. This allows students to compare their writing with the model. (visual, kinesthetic)

Featured Letters

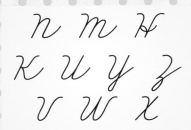

Featured Key to Legibility:

Students will consider **size** as they evaluate their writing.

Other Acceptable Letterforms

These are acceptable variations of the models in this book.

Teaching the Letters:
Legibility

The teacher may help the students transfer good handwriting to writing in the content areas by recognizing and valuing legibility in all written work. When their handwriting is regularly evaluated, students will begin to make a habit of remembering the four Keys—shape, size, spacing, and slant—whenever they write. As they gain automaticity in their handwriting, students are free to focus on what they want to communicate, rather than on the mechanics of the communication.

Write Curve Forward Letters

You will learn to write these uppercase letters. Each letter begins with a curve forward stroke.

Trace and write curve forward-slant strokes.

Keys to Legibility
Make your writing easy to read. As you write curve forward letters, you will pay attention to the size of your writing.

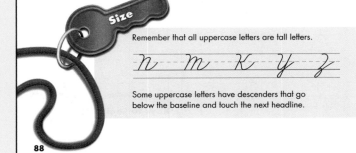

Remember that all uppercase letters are tall letters.

Some uppercase letters have descenders that go below the baseline and touch the next headline.

88

1. Present the Letters

Point out the uppercase letters on the page, and explain that each one begins with a curve forward stroke. In most of the letters, the curve forward is followed by a slant stroke. Encourage students to use their finger or a pencil to trace several of the curve forward strokes in these letters. Then have them trace and write the curve forward-slant strokes on the guidelines.

Direct the students to notice the stop-and-check symbol at the end of the writing grid. Guide them in choosing and circling their best stroke.

2. Present the Key

Point out the Key feature on the student page. This Key helps them consider the size of their writing as they evaluate legibility.

What the research says . . .

Findings revealed significantly higher scores for neatly handwritten essays; no differences were found between typed and poorly handwritten ones. Regardless of rater training and essay quality, essays were much more likely to receive higher grades if they were neatly handwritten.

—C. Sweedler-Brown, "Computers and assessment: The effect of typing versus handwriting on the holistic scoring of essays." *Journal of Research and Development in Education,* 26(1)

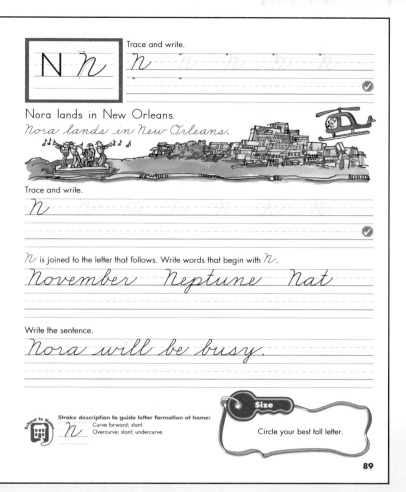

Trace and write.

N n   n   n   n   n   n   ✓

Nora lands in New Orleans.
Nora lands in New Orleans.

Trace and write.
n   n   n   n   n   ✓

n is joined to the letter that follows. Write words that begin with n.
November   Neptune   Nat

Write the sentence.
Nora will be busy.

Stroke description to guide letter formation at home:
n   Curve forward; slant.
    Overcurve; slant; undercurve.

Size
Circle your best tall letter.

89

- Curve forward, slant
- Overcurve, slant, under-curve

Coaching Hint

Increasing Speed Tell students they can increase their handwriting speed through meaningful practice. Do not draw the letters. (visual)

---

1 Present the Letter

Help students focus on the letter **N** by asking:
- What stroke follows the first slant? *(overcurve)*
- How many slant strokes are in **N**? *(two)*

Model Write **N** on guidelines as you say the stroke description. Model writing **N** in the air as you repeat the stroke description. Have students say the words as they use their index finger to write large **N**'s on the chalkboard.

Corrective Strategy
Make sure the overcurve is round.

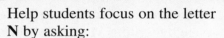
n   not   n

2 Write and Evaluate

After students have practiced writing **N** on scrap paper or practice boards, ask them to trace and write the first row of letters.

Stop and Check To help students evaluate **N**, ask:
- Are your slant strokes pulled toward the baseline?
- Is your overcurve round?

Families may use the stroke description on the student page to encourage good letter formation at home. **Practice Master 98** provides take-home practice for the letters **E** and **N**.

3 Apply

Ask students to complete the page by writing **N** and the words and sentence. Remind students to think about size as they write, remembering that tall letters touch the headline, but short letters never go above the midline.

PRACTICE MASTER 52

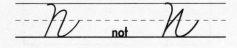

- Curve forward, slant
- Overcurve, slant
- Overcurve, slant, undercurve

Coaching Hint

Paper Position To ensure correct paper placement, position the paper properly at the correct height on the desk for each student and use tape to create a frame on the desk around each corner of the paper. The student will now be able to place the paper in the correct position. (kinesthetic, visual)

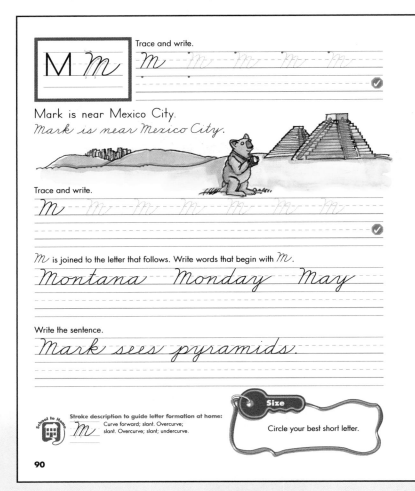

M m — Trace and write.

Mark is near Mexico City.
Mark is near Mexico City.

Trace and write.

M is joined to the letter that follows. Write words that begin with *M*.

Montana   Monday   May

Write the sentence.

Mark sees pyramids.

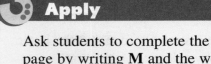
Stroke description to guide letter formation at home:
M Curve forward; slant. Overcurve; slant. Overcurve; slant; undercurve.

Size
Circle your best short letter.

90

---

1. Present the Letter

Help students focus on the letter **M** by asking:
- How many slant strokes are in **M**? *(three)*
- Where does **M** end? *(at the midline)*

Model Write **M** on guidelines as you say the stroke description. Model writing **M** in the air as you repeat the stroke description. Have students say the words as they use their index finger to write large **M**'s on their desktop.

Corrective Strategy
Pause after the first and second slant strokes.

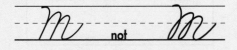

2. Write and Evaluate

After students have practiced writing **M** on scrap paper or practice boards, ask them to trace and write the first row of letters.

 Stop and Check To help students evaluate **M,** ask:
- Does your **M** end at the midline?
- Is your second overcurve shorter than your first?

Families may use the stroke description on the student page to encourage good letter formation at home. **Practice Master 99** provides take-home practice for the letters **M** and **H**.

3. Apply

Ask students to complete the page by writing **M** and the words and sentence. Remind students to think about size as they write, remembering to make their letters the same height as the models.

PRACTICE MASTER 53

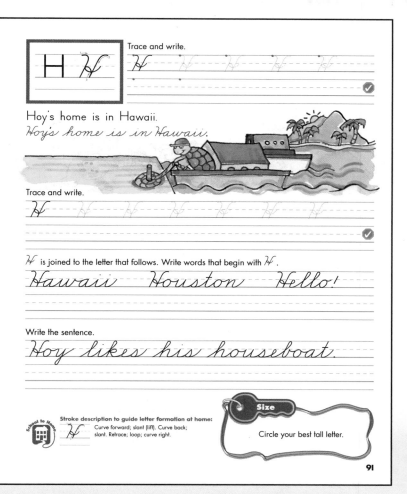

H H   Trace and write.

Hoy's home is in Hawaii.
Hoy's home is in Hawaii.

Trace and write.
H

H is joined to the letter that follows. Write words that begin with H.
Hawaii   Houston   Hello!

Write the sentence.
Hoy likes his houseboat.

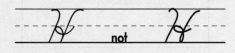
Stroke description to guide letter formation at home:
H Curve forward; slant (lift). Curve back;
slant. Retrace; loop; curve right.

Size
Circle your best tall letter.

91

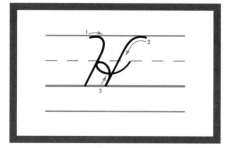

• Curve forward, slant, (lift)
• Curve back, slant
• Retrace, loop, curve right

Coaching Hint

Hands-On Writing Provide a small amount of shaving cream, a drop of tempera paint, and a paper plate for each student. Direct the students to mix the shaving cream and paint with their fingertips and to practice the strokes, joinings, and letters you call out. (auditory, kinesthetic)

1. Present the Letter

Help students focus on the letter **H** by asking:
• How many loops are in **H**? *(one)*
• How many lifts are in **H**? *(one)*

Model Write **H** on guidelines as you say the stroke description. Model writing **H** in the air as you repeat the stroke description. Have students say the description as they write **H** in the air with you.

Corrective Strategy

Retrace before the loop.

H   **not**   H

2. Write and Evaluate

After students have practiced writing **H** on scrap paper or practice boards, ask them to trace and write the first row of letters.

 Stop and Check To help students evaluate **H**, ask:
• Is your **H** about the same width as the model?
• Does your loop touch the first slant stroke at the midline, and is it a slanted loop?

School to Home

Families may use the stroke description on the student page to encourage good letter formation at home. **Practice Master 99** provides take-home practice for the letters **M** and **H**.

3. Apply

Ask students to complete the page by writing **H** and the words and sentence. Remind students to write letters with consistent and correct size.

PRACTICE MASTER 54

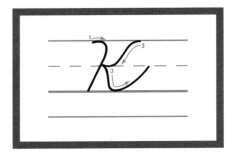

- Curve forward, slant, (lift)
- Doublecurve
- Curve forward and down, undercurve

Coaching Hint

Left-Handed Writers Students can be grouped together for handwriting instruction at the chalkboard as well as at their desks. While writing at the chalkboard, they can practice keeping their hand below the line of writing. *(visual, kinesthetic)*

Trace and write.

Keiko hikes in King's Canyon.
Keiko hikes in King's Canyon.

Trace and write.

$\mathcal{K}$ is joined to the letter that follows. Write words that begin with $\mathcal{K}$.

Kansas   Kentucky   Ken

Write the sentence.

Keep on the trail, Keiko!

 Stroke description to guide letter formation at home:
Curve forward; slant (lift).
Doublecurve. Curve forward and down; undercurve.

Size Circle your best short letter.

92

---

1. Present the Letter

Help students focus on the letter **K** by asking:
- Where is the lift in **K**? *(after the slant)*
- What stroke follows the lift? *(doublecurve)*

Model Write **K** on guidelines as you say the stroke description. Model writing **K** in the air as you repeat the stroke description. Have students say the description as they use their index finger to write large **K**'s on the chalkboard.

Corrective Strategy

Curve forward and down before the undercurve ending.

 not

2. Write and Evaluate

After students have practiced writing **K** on scrap paper or practice boards, ask them to trace and write the first row of letters.

✓ **Stop and Check** To help students evaluate **K,** ask:
- Does your **K** rest on the baseline?
- Does your **K** end at the midline?

Families may use the stroke description on the student page to encourage good letter formation at home. **Practice Master 100** provides take-home practice for the letters **K** and **U**.

3. Apply

Ask students to complete the page by writing **K** and the words and sentence. Remind students to compare the size of their letters with the models.

PRACTICE MASTER 55

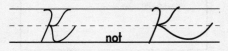

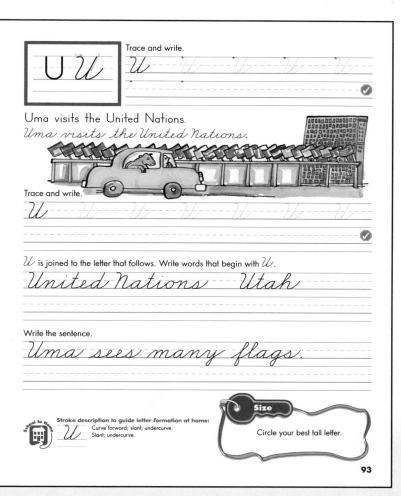

Trace and write.

U U

Uma visits the United Nations.
Uma visits the United Nations.

Trace and write.

𝒰

𝒰 is joined to the letter that follows. Write words that begin with 𝒰.

United Nations   Utah

Write the sentence.

Uma sees many flags.

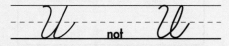

Stroke description to guide letter formation at home:
𝒰   Curve forward; slant; undercurve.
     Slant; undercurve.

Size

Circle your best tall letter.

93

- Curve forward, slant, undercurve
- Slant, undercurve

Coaching Hint

Writing Lines Review with students the use of guidelines for correct letter formation. Draw guidelines on the chalkboard, using colored chalk to identify the headline, midline, and baseline. Invite volunteers to write words on the guidelines. (visual, auditory, kinesthetic)

---

1 Present the Letter

Help students focus on the letter **U** by asking:

- How many undercurves are in **U**? *(two)*
- Where does the first undercurve end? *(at the headline)*

Model Write **U** on guidelines as you say the stroke description. Model writing **U** in the air as you repeat the stroke description. Have students say the words as they use their index finger to write large **U**'s on their desktop.

Corrective Strategy

Pause before retracing to write the second slant stroke.

𝒰   not   𝒰

2 Write and Evaluate

After students have practiced writing **U** on scrap paper or practice boards, ask them to trace and write the first row of letters.

 Stop and Check To help students evaluate **U,** ask:

- Do your slant strokes have the proper slant?
- Does your **U** rest on the baseline?

Families may use the stroke description on the student page to encourage good letter formation at home. **Practice Master 100** provides take-home practice for the letters **K** and **U**.

3 Apply

Ask students to complete the page by writing **U** and the words and sentence. Remind students to think about size as they write, remembering to use the guidelines to help them form letters that are the proper height.

PRACTICE MASTER 56

- Curve forward, slant, undercurve
- Slant, loop back, overcurve

Coaching Hint

Pencil Position Holding the pencil too tightly causes a student to tire easily when writing. To overcome this problem, have the student crumple a piece of paper, place it in the palm of the writing hand, and pick up the pencil. This will serve as a reminder not to squeeze the pencil. (kinesthetic)

Trace and write.

Y Y *Y Y Y Y Y*

Yogi is in Yellowstone Park.
Yogi is in Yellowstone Park.

Trace and write.

Y Y Y Y Y Y

Y is joined to the letter that follows. Write words that begin with *Y*.

Yellowstone   Yorktown

Write the sentences.

Yikes! Yogi, be careful!

Stroke description to guide letter formation at home:
Y Curve forward; slant; undercurve.
Slant; loop back; overcurve.

Size Circle your best letter that has a descender.

94

---

1. Present the Letter

Help students focus on the letter **Y** by asking:
- How does **Y** end? *(with an overcurve)*
- Where does the loop close? *(near the baseline)*

Model Write **Y** on guidelines as you say the stroke description. Model writing **Y** in the air as you repeat the stroke description. Have students say the words as they use their index finger to write large **Y**'s on their desktop.

Corrective Strategy
Pause after the undercurve, to avoid looping.

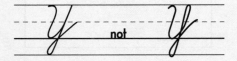
Y not *Y*

T94

2. Write and Evaluate

After students have practiced writing **Y** on scrap paper or practice boards, ask them to trace and write the first row of letters.

✔ **Stop and Check** To help students evaluate **Y,** ask:
- Is your **Y** about the same size as the model?
- Does your loop close near the baseline?

Families may use the stroke description on the student page to encourage good letter formation at home. **Practice Master 101** provides take-home practice for the letters **Y** and **Z**.

3. Apply

Ask students to complete the page by writing **Y** and the words and sentences. Remind students to check the size of their letters by comparing them with the models, remembering that letters with descenders touch the headline of the next writing space.

PRACTICE MASTER 57

Name:

Write the letter and the words.

Y   Y Y Y Y Y
Y   Y Y Y Y Y
Yonkers   Yorktown
Yelena   Yolonda   Yvette

Write the sentences.
Yasmine works in Yemen.
Yoshi went to New York.

Copyright © Zaner-Bloser, Inc.   Practice Master 57

Student Page

Trace and write.

Z Z

Zack raced to Zion National Park.
Zack raced to Zion National Park.

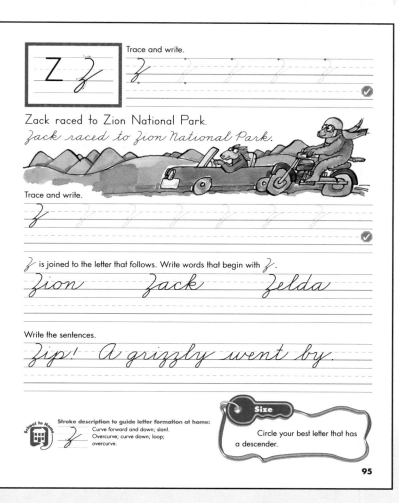

Trace and write.

Z

Z is joined to the letter that follows. Write words that begin with Z.

Zion   Zack   Zelda

Write the sentences.

Zip! A grizzly went by.

Size

Circle your best letter that has a descender.

95

- Curve forward and down, slant
- Overcurve, curve down, loop, overcurve

Coaching Hint

Keys to Legibility Remind students that the four Keys to Legibility—shape, size, spacing, and slant—form a rubric for evaluating handwriting. The Keys can be used to consistently evaluate and improve handwriting in all subject areas.

---

1 Present the Letter

Help students focus on the letter **Z** by asking:

- How many loops are in **Z**? *(one)*
- How does **Z** end? *(with an overcurve)*

Model Write **Z** on guidelines as you say the stroke description. Model writing **Z** in the air as you repeat the stroke description. Have students say the description as they take turns dipping their finger in water and writing **Z** on the chalkboard.

Corrective Strategy

The curve forward and down and the slant should flow smoothly.

Z **not** Z

2 Write and Evaluate

After students have practiced writing **Z** on scrap paper or practice boards, ask them to trace and write the first row of letters.

Stop and Check To help students evaluate **Z,** ask:

- Does your loop close near the baseline?
- Do your strokes look like the model?

Families may use the stroke description on the student page to encourage good letter formation at home. **Practice Master 101** provides take-home practice for the letters **Y** and **Z**.

3 Apply

Ask students to complete the page by writing **Z** and the words and sentences. Remind students that it is important to make each letter the correct size, including letters with descenders.

PRACTICE MASTER 58

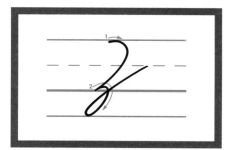

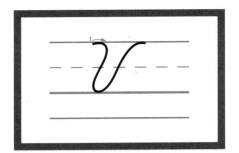

- Curve forward, slant, undercurve, overcurve

Coaching Hint

Improving Size Demonstrate drawing a horizontal line with a ruler along the tops of letters to show proper size. Students who have difficulty with correct size of letters may benefit from writing on paper with wide guidelines. (kinesthetic, visual)

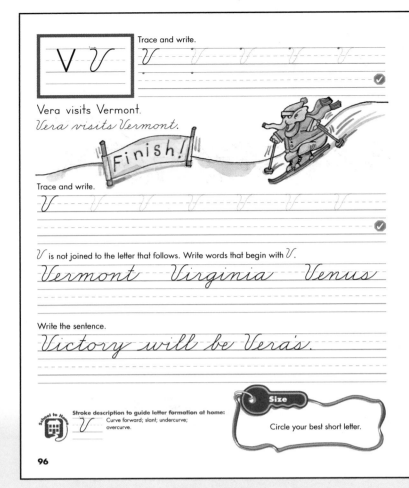

Trace and write.

V V

Vera visits Vermont.
Vera visits Vermont.

Trace and write.

$\mathcal{V}$ is not joined to the letter that follows. Write words that begin with $\mathcal{V}$.

Vermont   Virginia   Venus

Write the sentence.

Victory will be Vera's.

Stroke description to guide letter formation at home: Curve forward; slant; undercurve; overcurve.

Size
Circle your best short letter.

96

---

1. Present the Letter

Help students focus on the letter **V** by asking:
- How does **V** begin? *(with a curve forward, slant)*
- Where does **V** end? *(just below the headline)*

Model Write **V** on guidelines as you say the stroke description. Model writing **V** in the air as you repeat the stroke description. Have students say the description as they write **V** in the air with you.

Corrective Strategy
Make sure the bottom is round.

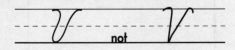

V not V

2. Write and Evaluate

After students have practiced writing **V** on scrap paper or practice boards, ask them to trace and write the first row of letters.

Stop and Check To help students evaluate **V,** ask:
- Is your **V** about the same width as the model?
- Is the bottom round?

School to Home

Families may use the stroke description on the student page to encourage good letter formation at home. **Practice Master 102** provides take-home practice for the letters **V** and **W.**

3. Apply

Ask students to complete the page by writing **V** and the words and sentence. Remind students to write with consistent and correct size so their letters will be easy to read.

PRACTICE MASTER 59

Name:
Write the letter and the words.

V V V V V
V V V V V

Vail   Vermont   Vista
Vanida   Vivica   Viv

Write the sentences.
Val lives in Vienna

Viv moved to Vineland

Copyright © Zaner-Bloser, Inc.   Practice Master 59

Student Page (top left)

Trace and write.

W W   W

Walt likes Washington, D.C.
Walt likes Washington, D.C.

Trace and write.

W

W is not joined to the letter that follows. Write words that begin with *W*.

Washington   Wednesday

Write the sentence.

Walt watches a parade!

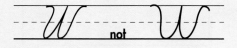

Stroke description to guide letter formation at home:
W   Curve forward; slant; undercurve.
     Slant; undercurve; overcurve.

Size

Circle your best tall letter.

97

- Curve forward, slant, undercurve
- Slant, undercurve, over-curve

Coaching Hint

Increasing Speed Writing rate will increase as students begin to move the writing hand more freely. Have students practice writing letters and words in a large size with crayon on folded newsprint to encourage free movement of the arm and hand. (kinesthetic)

---

1. Present the Letter

Help students focus on the letter **W** by asking:

- Where does **W** begin? (*just below the headline*)
- How many undercurves are in **W**? (*two*)

Model Write **W** on guidelines as you say the stroke description. Model writing **W** in the air as you repeat the stroke description. Have students say the description as they use their finger to write large **W**'s on their desktop.

Corrective Strategy

Say each stroke as you write the letter.

W   not   W

2. Write and Evaluate

After students have practiced writing **W** on scrap paper or practice boards, ask them to trace and write the first row of letters.

Stop and Check To help students evaluate **W,** ask:

- Is your **W** about the same width as the model?
- Does your **W** touch the headline three times?

School to Home

Families may use the stroke description on the student page to encourage good letter formation at home. **Practice Master 102** provides take-home practice for the letters **V** and **W**.

3. Apply

Ask students to complete the page by writing **W** and the words and sentence. Remind students to think about size as they write, remembering that tall letters touch the headline and short letters touch the midline.

PRACTICE MASTER 60

Name:

Write the letter and the words.

W   W W W W W
W W W W W W W

Wabash   Wales   Wichita
Wilma   Wong   Wilson

Write the sentences.
Wes is in Washington.
We are in Winnipeg.

Practice Master 60   Copyright © Zaner-Bloser, Inc.

- Curve forward, slant, undercurve, (lift)
- Slant

Coaching Hint

Hands-On Writing Write letters on pieces of poster board or cardboard and laminate them. Students can use them as a base to form letters with clay. (kinesthetic, visual)

Trace and write.

Xena dreamed of Planet X.
Xena dreamed of Planet X.

Trace and write.

X is not joined to the letter that follows. Write words that begin with *X*.

Xena   Xanadu   X-ray

Write the sentence.

Xena was excited.

Stroke description to guide letter formation at home:
X Curve forward; slant; undercurve (lift). Slant.

Size
Circle your best short letter.

98

---

1. Present the Letter

Help students focus on the letter **X** by asking:
- How does **X** begin? *(with a curve forward)*
- Where is the lift? *(after the undercurve)*

Model Write **X** on guidelines as you say the stroke description. Model writing **X** in the air as you repeat the stroke description. Have students say the description as they write **X** in the air with you.

Corrective Strategy
The second slant stroke crosses the first near the midline.

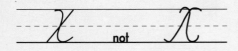

2. Write and Evaluate

After students have practiced writing **X** on scrap paper or practice boards, ask them to trace and write the first row of letters.

Stop and Check To help students evaluate **X**, ask:
- Does your **X** rest on the baseline?
- Are your curve strokes smooth?

Families may use the stroke description on the student page to encourage good letter formation at home. **Practice Master 103** provides take-home practice for the letters **X** and **I**.

3. Apply

Ask students to complete the page by writing **X** and the words and sentence. Remind students to think about size as they write, remembering that correct size helps make handwriting easy to read.

PRACTICE MASTER 61

T98

Practice

n m H K U

Y Z V W X

Here are titles of books you may have read.
Write the titles. Underline them.

Under My Nose

When We Were Very Young

17 Kings and 42 Elephants

Henry Huggins

Zella, Zack, and Zodiac

99

Review the Letters

Direct the students to look at the letters being reviewed on student page 99. Ask them what they remember about the shape of these letters. (*All begin with a curve forward stroke.*)

Review the stroke descriptions and model again any of the letters the students may be having difficulty writing.

Ask a volunteer to give a verbal description of one of these letters: **N, M, H, K, U, Y, Z, V, W, X.** Challenge the other students to identify the letter being described and then write it on guidelines on the chalkboard.

Write and Evaluate

Read the directions on student page 99 with the students. Point out that handwritten book titles are underlined. Have the students write the titles on the page, remembering to form letters with correct shape and size.

✓ **Stop and Check** To help students evaluate their writing, ask:

- Did you underline the book titles?
- Did you write with correct strokes so your letters have good shape?
- Did you use the guidelines to make letters with correct size?
- Do your short letters touch both the midline and the baseline?
- Do your tall letters touch both the headline and the baseline?
- Do your short letters with descenders touch the headline of the next writing space?

Corrective Strategy

Extend the curve right to connect to the next letter.

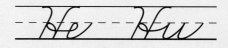

More About Practice

Make handwriting practice fun and memorable by including a variety of activities; for example: finger-tracing on their palms or on a partner's back; writing on a Magna Doodle, magic slate, or similar toy; finger-writing in paint or shaving cream; writing with markers in a large size on chart paper; writing letters using the drawing tool in a favorite software program.

Application

Henry Huggins meets a funny dog. He likes the dog right away. While on their way to Henry's house, they have lots of adventures. What a great book! You should read it.

Complete this book review in *cursive* handwriting.

Title: Henry Huggins
Author: Beverly Cleary
What Happened:

Keys to Legibility

My writing has good shape. ☐
My writing has good size. ☐

100

Apply

Read the directions on student page 100 with the students and review the book review. Then have the students complete the book review in cursive handwriting. Remind them to write carefully and to use the guidelines to form letters with proper shape and correct size.

Help students summarize what they have learned about shape and size. Then have them respond to the checklist in the Key feature.

Self Evaluation

Self-evaluation is important in the handwriting process. By identifying their strengths and weaknesses, students become independent learners. Here are the steps in the self-evaluation process:

Question
Students should ask themselves questions such as "Is my slant correct?" "Do my letters rest on the baseline?"

Compare
Students should compare their handwriting to correct models.

Evaluate
Students should determine strengths and weaknesses in their handwriting based on the Keys to Legibility.

Diagnose
Students should diagnose the cause of any difficulties. Possible causes include incorrect paper or pencil position, inconsistent pressure on the pencil, and incorrect strokes.

Improve
Self-evaluation should include a means of improvement through additional instruction and continued practice.

Special Helps
Maureen King
Occupational Therapist

This activity will help students refine wrist, thumb, and finger interaction as well as support hand-eye coordination. Have students hold a rubber pencil topper with the thumb and index finger of each hand (make sure thumbs are on top). Using the open ends of the toppers, grip cubes or small counting blocks, one at a time, and stack—and unstack. Goal is ten cubes.

T100

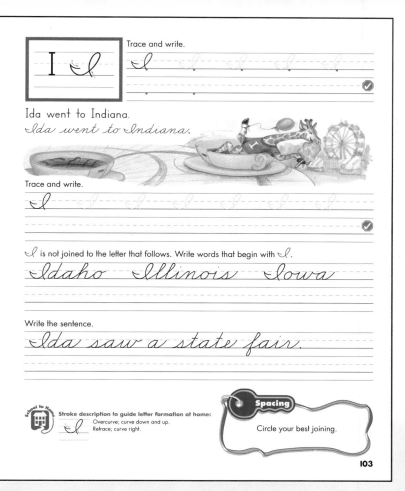

Trace and write.

Ida went to Indiana.
Ida went to Indiana.

Trace and write.

 is not joined to the letter that follows. Write words that begin with .

Idaho   Illinois   Iowa

Write the sentence.

Ida saw a state fair.

Spacing
Circle your best joining.

103

- Overcurve, curve down and up
- Retrace, curve right

Coaching Hint

Practice If students have not mastered a particular handwriting skill, provide additional instruction and practice. Reinforce instruction with activities geared to each student's modality strengths (visual, auditory, or kinesthetic). Help them evaluate their writing.

1. Present the Letter

Help students focus on the letter **I** by asking:
- Where does **I** begin? (*just below the baseline*)
- Where is the pause in **I**? (*at the midline before the retrace*)

Model Write **I** on guidelines as you say the stroke description. Model writing **I** in the air as you repeat the stroke description. Have students echo the description as they write **I** in the air with you.

Corrective Strategy

Pause after the curve at the midline and retrace.

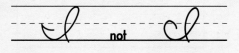

2. Write and Evaluate

After students have practiced writing **I** on scrap paper or practice boards, ask them to trace and write the first row of letters.

 Stop and Check To help students evaluate **I**, ask:
- Does your **I** begin just below the baseline?
- Is the slant of your **I** correct?

School to Home

Families may use the stroke description on the student page to encourage good letter formation at home. **Practice Master 103** provides take-home practice for the letters **X** and **I**.

3. Apply

Ask students to complete the page by writing **I** and the words and sentence. Remind students to think about spacing as they write, remembering to leave consistent space after uppercase letters that don't join with the next letter.

PRACTICE MASTER 62

T103

• Overcurve, slant, loop back, overcurve

Coaching Hint

Handwriting Tip Have students use a pencil with #2 or softer lead. Make sure students do not apply a lot of pressure to their pencils as they write. (kinesthetic)

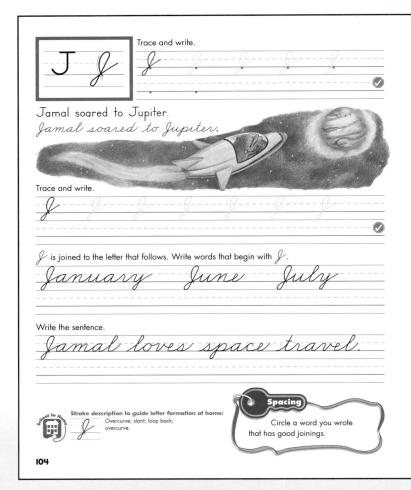

J J Trace and write.

Jamal soared to Jupiter.
Jamal soared to Jupiter.

Trace and write.

J is joined to the letter that follows. Write words that begin with *J*.

January   June   July

Write the sentence.
Jamal loves space travel.

Stroke description to guide letter formation at home:
J Overcurve; slant; loop back; overcurve.

Spacing
Circle a word you wrote that has good joinings.

104

---

1. Present the Letter

Help students focus on the letter **J** by asking:
- Where does **J** begin? (*just below the baseline*)
- Where do the two loops close? (*near the baseline*)

Model Write **J** on guidelines as you say the stroke description. Model writing **J** in the air as you repeat the stroke description. Have students say the words as they use their index finger to write large **J**'s in shaving cream on their desktop.

Corrective Strategy

Make sure the descender is long enough.

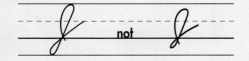
J **not** *J*

2. Write and Evaluate

After students have practiced writing **J** on scrap paper or practice boards, ask them to trace and write the first row of letters.

 Stop and Check To help students evaluate **J**, ask:
- Do your loops close near the baseline?
- Does your first overcurve touch the headline?

School to Home

Families may use the stroke description on the student page to encourage good letter formation at home. **Practice Master 104** provides take-home practice for the letters **J** and **Q**.

3. Apply

Ask students to complete the page by writing **J** and the words and sentence. Remind students to think about spacing as they write, following the spacing in the models.

PRACTICE MASTER 63

Name:

Write the letter and the words.

J   J   J   J   J   J
J   J   J   J   J
Jackson   Joliet   Japan
Jett   Jay   Jolynn

Write the sentences.
Jasmine jets to Joplin.
Jake is in Jordan.

Copyright © Zaner-Bloser, Inc.   Practice Master 63

Trace and write.

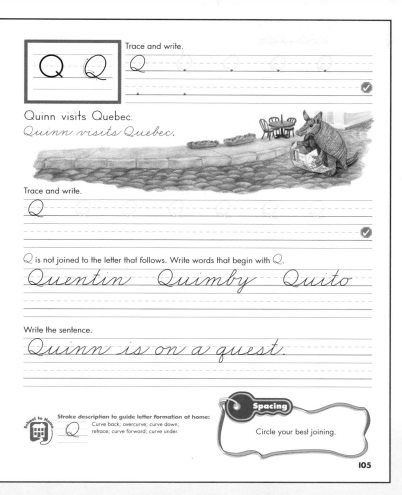

Q Q   Q

Quinn visits Quebec.
Quinn visits Quebec.

Trace and write.

Q

Q is not joined to the letter that follows. Write words that begin with Q.

Quentin Quimby Quito

Write the sentence.

Quinn is on a quest.

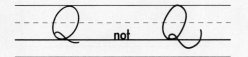

Stroke description to guide letter formation at home:
Q   Curve back; overcurve; curve down;
retrace; curve forward; curve under.

Spacing

Circle your best joining.

105

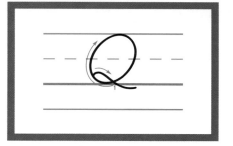

Q

- Curve back, overcurve, curve down, retrace, curve forward, curve under

Coaching Hint

Left-Handed Writers

Encourage students to practice their handwriting skills with other left-handed writers. Boost students' confidence by explaining that "lefties" make up 10–15% of the population. Famous left-handers include Albert Einstein, Babe Ruth, and Oprah Winfrey.

---

1. Present the Letter

Help students focus on the letter **Q** by asking:
- Where does **Q** begin? *(at the baseline)*
- How does **Q** end? *(with a curve under)*

Model Write **Q** on guidelines as you say the stroke description. Model writing **Q** in the air as you repeat the stroke description. Have students say the words as they use their index finger to write large **Q**'s on their desktop.

Corrective Strategy

The curve under stroke ends below the baseline.

Q   not   Q

2. Write and Evaluate

After students have practiced writing **Q** on scrap paper or practice boards, ask them to trace and write the first row of letters.

✓ **Stop and Check** To help students evaluate **Q**, ask:
- Does your **Q** begin at the baseline?
- Is your **Q** closed?

School to Home

Families may use the stroke description on the student page to encourage good letter formation at home. **Practice Master 104** provides take-home practice for the letters **J** and **Q**.

3. Apply

Ask students to complete the page by writing **Q** and the words and sentence. Remind students to think about spacing as they write, remembering that consistent and proper spacing makes their writing easy to read.

PRACTICE MASTER 64

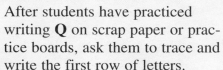

Name:

Write the letter and the words.

Q   Q Q Q Q Q
Q Q Q Q Q Q
Quietta Quatar Queens
Quito Quincy Quinn

Write the sentences.
I am not near Quebec.

Quit going to Quena.

Practice Master 64   Copyright © Zaner-Bloser, Inc.

T105

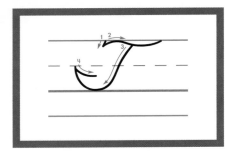

- Slant
- Curve forward and right, (lift)
- Doublecurve, curve up
- Retrace, curve right

Coaching Hint

Seeing Improvement If students can see improvement, they will be encouraged to try harder. Have them compare their writing now with earlier samples to note the improvements. (visual)

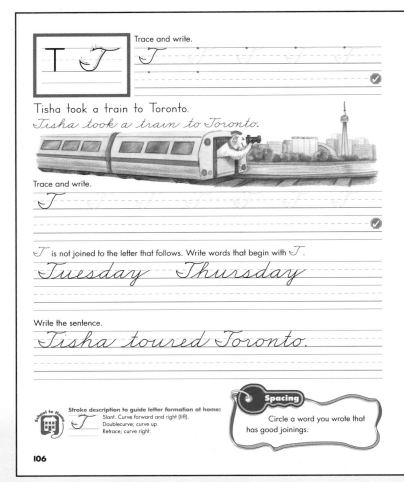

Trace and write.

Tisha took a train to Toronto.
Tisha took a train to Toronto.

Trace and write.

$\mathcal{T}$ is not joined to the letter that follows. Write words that begin with $\mathcal{T}$.
Tuesday   Thursday

Write the sentence.
Tisha toured Toronto.

Stroke description to guide letter formation at home:
Slant. Curve forward and right (lift).
Doublecurve; curve up.
Retrace; curve right.

Spacing
Circle a word you wrote that has good joinings.

106

 Present the Letter

Help students focus on the letter **T** by asking:
- Where does **T** begin? *(at the headline)*
- What is the first stroke in **T**? *(slant)*

Model Write **T** on guidelines as you say the stroke description. Model writing **T** in the air as you repeat the stroke description. Have students say the description as they write **T** in the air with you.

Corrective Strategy
The last stroke curves right.

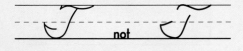

 Write and Evaluate

After students have practiced writing **T** on scrap paper or practice boards, ask them to trace and write the first row of letters.

Stop and Check To help students evaluate **T**, ask:
- Does your **T** begin at the headline?
- Does your last stroke curve right?

School to Home

Families may use the stroke description on the student page to encourage good letter formation at home. **Practice Master 105** provides take-home practice for the letters **T** and **F**.

 Apply

Ask students to complete the page by writing **T** and the words and sentence. Remind students to think about spacing as they write, leaving room for a short slant stroke between words in a sentence.

PRACTICE MASTER 65

Name:
Write the letter and the words.
T T T T T
T T T T T T
Tacoma Tampa Tonga
Tate Thor Tess
Write the sentences.
Tori toured Tulsa.
I went to Turkey.

Copyright © Zaner-Bloser, Inc.   Practice Master 65

TI06

Trace and write.

F F F

Fred flew to Florida.
Fred flew to Florida.

Trace and write.

F F F

F is not joined to the letter that follows. Write words that begin with F.

Flint   Friday   February

Write the sentence.

Fred found a friend.

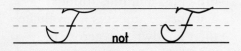
Stroke description to guide letter formation at home:
Slant. Curve forward and right (lift).
Doublecurve; curve up.
Retrace; curve right (lift). Slide right.

Spacing
Circle your best joining.

107

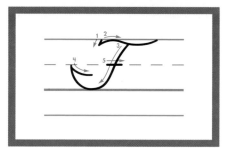

- Slant
- Curve forward and right, (lift)
- Doublecurve, curve up
- Retrace, curve right, (lift)
- Slide right

Coaching Hint

Pencil Position Students will benefit from the use of the Zaner-Bloser *Writing Frame* to foster correct hand position and arm movement. (kinesthetic)

---

1 Present the Letter

Help students focus on the letter **F** by asking:
- How are **T** and **F** alike? (*There is a T in F.*)
- How are they different? (*In F, the last stroke is a slide right.*)

Model Write **F** on guidelines as you say the stroke description. Model writing **F** in the air as you repeat the stroke description. Have students say the words as they dip their index finger in water and write large **F**'s on the chalkboard.

Corrective Strategy
Pause before the retrace.

F not *F*

2 Write and Evaluate

After students have practiced writing **F** on scrap paper or practice boards, ask them to trace and write the first row of letters.

 Stop and Check To help students evaluate **F**, ask:
- Does your **F** rest on the baseline?
- Is your slide right stroke at the midline?

School to Home

Families may use the stroke description on the student page to encourage good letter formation at home. **Practice Master 105** provides take-home practice for the letters **T** and **F**.

3 Apply

Ask students to complete the page by writing **F** and the words and sentence. Remind students to think about spacing as they write, remembering to leave consistent and proper space between letters and between words.

PRACTICE MASTER 66

Name

Write the letter and the words.
F F F F F
F F F F F F

Fargo   Fiji   Flint
Fajim   Fannie   Fletch

Write the sentences.
Fran flew to Findlay

Is Frisco in Franklin?

Practice Master 66   Copyright © Zaner-Bloser, Inc.

T107

Practice

Practice

I J Q T F

Write the sentence.

I read about presidents.

Write these names of American presidents.

Third President: *Thomas Jefferson*

Sixth President: *John Quincy Adams*

Tenth President: *John Tyler*

Thirteenth President: *Millard Fillmore*

108

Review the Letters

Direct the students to look at the letters being reviewed on student page 108. Ask them what they remember about the shape of these letters. (*I and J begin with an overcurve; Q begins with a curve back and an overcurve; T and F contain a doublecurve.*)

Review the stroke descriptions and model again any of the letters the students may be having difficulty writing.

Ask a volunteer to give a verbal description of one of these letters: **I, J, Q, T, F**. Challenge the other students to identify the letter being described and then write it on guidelines on the chalkboard.

Write and Evaluate

Have the students write the sentence and the names of the presidents on the page, remembering to form letters with correct shape and size and to use good spacing.

 Stop and Check To help students evaluate their writing, ask:

- Did you write with correct strokes so your letters have good shape?
- Did you use the guidelines to make letters with correct size?
- Do your short letters touch both the midline and the baseline?
- Do your tall letters touch both the headline and the baseline?
- Do your short letters with descenders touch the headline of the next writing space?
- Are your letters and words written with good spacing?

Corrective Strategy

Refer to the models to judge the spacing between letters that do not connect.

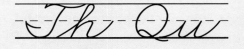

More About Practice

Students who are learning how to write need a variety of meaningful ways to use their new skills. Ask them to practice handwriting as they fill in classroom forms, make lists of things to do, practice writing spelling words, and label drawings and illustrations. Encourage students to evaluate their handwriting across the curriculum—not just during "handwriting time."

T108

Application
Writing Facts

Jupiter is a large planet.
Fixed stars are far off.
Io is a moon of Jupiter.
The sun is just a star.
Earth has one moon.
Quasars are big and shiny.

Write the facts about space in *cursive* handwriting.

Keys to Legibility
My writing has good shape. ☐
My writing has good size. ☐
My writing has good spacing. ☐

109

Apply

Read the facts in the chart on student page 109 with the students. Then have them write the facts. Remind them to write carefully, to use the guidelines to help them form letters with proper shape and correct size, and to allow appropriate spacing between letters and between words.

Help students summarize what they have learned about shape, size, and spacing. Then have them respond to the checklist in the Key feature.

Special Helps
Maureen King
Occupational Therapist

Students who have difficulty with spacing, sequencing, and alignment of letters will benefit from activities designed to strengthen visual tracking. Cut apart the panels of a comic strip and ask students to use both hands to reassemble them in correct order. Alternately, ask students to write words on one-inch strips of paper. Then have partners put the word strips in order to make a sentence. Expand the activity by using sentence strips 6–8 inches long. This will prompt the other hand, as needed, to stabilize the paper.

Coaching Hint

Teaching Handwriting
Use a form of reciprocal teaching to reinforce correct formation of letters. Have students take turns demonstrating letter formation. Remind them to use correct terms and stroke descriptions and to refer to the writing lines. Teacher direction is important, but students should be encouraged to take the lead as much as possible. (visual, auditory)

Featured Letters

Featured Key to Legibility:

Students will consider **slant** as they evaluate their writing.

Other Acceptable Letterforms

These are acceptable variations of the models in this book.

Teaching the Letters:
Portfolio Assessment

A portfolio is an organized collection of a student's work. It is a tool for evaluation, reflection, and learning. A writing portfolio can demonstrate a student's progress toward the goal of legible handwriting. The student should use a combination of self-evaluation, peer evaluation, and teacher evaluation to select samples for the portfolio. Reviewing their portfolios at least once a week enables students to monitor their handwriting progress.

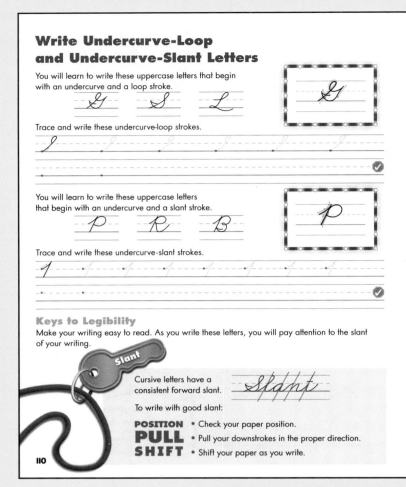

Write Undercurve-Loop and Undercurve-Slant Letters

You will learn to write these uppercase letters that begin with an undercurve and a loop stroke.

Trace and write these undercurve-loop strokes.

You will learn to write these uppercase letters that begin with an undercurve and a slant stroke.

Trace and write these undercurve-slant strokes.

Keys to Legibility

Make your writing easy to read. As you write these letters, you will pay attention to the slant of your writing.

Cursive letters have a consistent forward slant.

To write with good slant:

POSITION • Check your paper position.
PULL • Pull your downstrokes in the proper direction.
SHIFT • Shift your paper as you write.

110

1. Present the Letters

Point out the uppercase letters on the page, and explain that each letter in the first group begins with an undercurve-loop stroke and each in the next group begins with an undercurve-slant stroke. Have students trace and write the undercurve-loop and undercurve-slant strokes on the guidelines.

Direct the students to notice the stop-and-check symbol at the end of the writing grids. Guide the students in selecting and circling their best strokes.

2. Present the Key

Point out the Key feature on the student page. This Key helps them consider the slant of their writing as they evaluate legibility.

What the research says ...

For years, I have heard rumors about the demise of handwriting, as it would soon be replaced by word processing or speech synthesis (prior to that it was the typewriter). While these tools have clearly become a more prominent part of everyday life, handwriting has not been superseded.
—Steve Graham, *Handwriting Research and Resources: A Guide to Curriculum Planning*

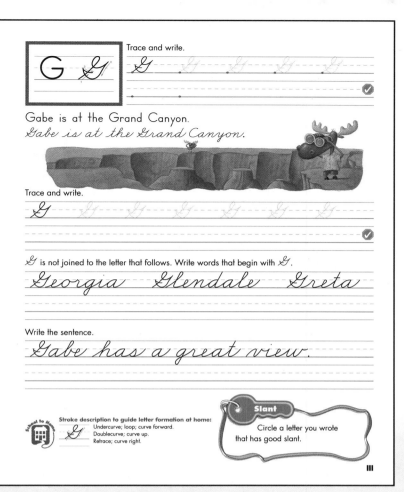

Trace and write.

Gabe is at the Grand Canyon.
Gabe is at the Grand Canyon.

Trace and write.

G is not joined to the letter that follows. Write words that begin with G.

Georgia   Glendale   Greta

Write the sentence.

Gabe has a great view.

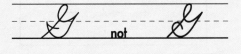
Stroke description to guide letter formation at home:
Undercurve; loop; curve forward.
Doublecurve; curve up.
Retrace; curve right.

Slant
Circle a letter you wrote that has good slant.

III

- Undercurve, loop, curve forward
- Doublecurve, curve up
- Retrace, curve right

Coaching Hint

Evaluating Slant Students can evaluate slant by drawing lines through the slant strokes of their letters. The lines should be parallel and should show the correct degree of forward slant. (visual, kinesthetic)

1. Present the Letter

Help students focus on the letter **G** by asking:

- Where does **G** begin? *(at the baseline)*
- Where does the retrace begin? *(at the midline)*

Model Write **G** on guidelines as you say the stroke description. Model writing **G** in the air as you repeat the stroke description. Have students echo the words as they use their index finger to write large **G**'s on their desktop.

Corrective Strategy
Pause before the retrace.

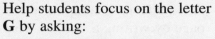
not

2. Write and Evaluate

After students have practiced writing **G** on scrap paper or practice boards, ask them to trace and write the first row of letters.

 Stop and Check To help students evaluate **G,** ask:

- Is your loop written from headline to midline?
- Is your **G** about the same width as the model?

School to Home

Families may use the stroke description on the student page to encourage good letter formation at home. **Practice Master 106** provides take-home practice for the letters **G** and **S**.

3. Apply

Ask students to complete the page by writing **G** and the words and sentence. Remind students to think about slant as they write, remembering to check the models often so their letters will be correct and easy to read.

PRACTICE MASTER 67

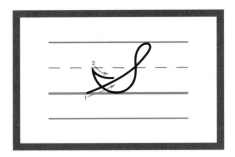

- Undercurve, loop, curve down and up
- Retrace, curve right

Trace and write.

S

Simone went to South Carolina.
Simone went to South Carolina.

Trace and write.

S is not joined to the letter that follows. Write words that begin with *S*.

Saturday Sunday Sam

Write the sentence.

Simone sat by the sea.

School to Home Stroke description to guide letter formation at home:
Undercurve; loop; curve down and up.
Retrace; curve right.

Slant
Circle a word you wrote that has good slant.

112

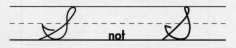

---

1. Present the Letter

Help students focus on the letter **S** by asking:
- Where does **S** begin? *(at the baseline)*
- How many loops are in **S**? *(one)*

Model Write **S** on guidelines as you say the stroke description. Model writing **S** in the air as you repeat the stroke description. Have students say the description as they write **S** in the air with you.

Corrective Strategy
Close the loop at the midline.

S   not   S

2. Write and Evaluate

After students have practiced writing **S** on scrap paper or practice boards, ask them to trace and write the first row of letters.

Stop and Check To help students evaluate **S,** ask:
- Does your **S** have correct slant?
- Does your curve right stop before the undercurve?

School to Home

Families may use the stroke description on the student page to encourage good letter formation at home. **Practice Master 106** provides take-home practice for the letters **G** and **S**.

3. Apply

Ask students to complete the page by writing **S** and the words and sentence. Remind students to think about slant as they write, remembering to pull their slant lines toward the baseline before beginning the next stroke.

PRACTICE MASTER 68

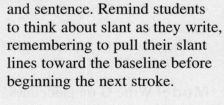

TII2

Trace and write.

L L $\mathcal{L}$ $\mathcal{L}$ $\mathcal{L}$ $\mathcal{L}$ $\mathcal{L}$

Lisa lives near Lake Erie.

Lisa lives near Lake Erie.

Trace and write.

$\mathcal{L}$ $\mathcal{L}$ $\mathcal{L}$ $\mathcal{L}$ $\mathcal{L}$ $\mathcal{L}$ $\mathcal{L}$

$\mathcal{L}$ is not joined to the letter that follows. Write words that begin with $\mathcal{L}$.

Louisiana   Little   League

Write the sentences.

Look! Lisa caught a log.

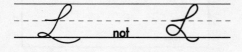
Stroke description to guide letter formation at home:
$\mathcal{L}$ Undercurve; loop; curve down; loop; curve under.

Slant
Circle a letter you wrote that has good slant.

113

- Undercurve, loop, curve down, loop, curve under

Coaching Hint

Evaluation Make students aware of their handwriting improvement by comparing their current writing with samples from the beginning of the year. This may provide motivation for further progress, particularly for students who have had difficulties with handwriting. (visual)

1. Present the Letter

Help students focus on the letter **L** by asking:
- How many loops are in **L**? *(two)*
- Where does **L** end? *(just below the baseline)*

Model Write **L** on guidelines as you say the stroke description. Model writing **L** in the air as you repeat the stroke description. Have students say the description as they use a paintbrush dipped in water to write **L** on the chalkboard.

Corrective Strategy
The lower loop is horizontal and rests on the baseline.

$\mathcal{L}$ **not** $\mathcal{L}$

2. Write and Evaluate

After students have practiced writing **L** on scrap paper or practice boards, ask them to trace and write the first row of letters.

 Stop and Check To help students evaluate **L,** ask:
- Does your **L** begin at the midline?
- Does your **L** end just below the baseline?

School to Home

Families may use the stroke description on the student page to encourage good letter formation at home. **Practice Master 107** provides take-home practice for the letters **L** and **P**.

3. Apply

Ask students to complete the page by writing **L** and the words and sentences. Remind students to think about slant as they write, remembering that consistent, forward slant makes their writing easier to read.

PRACTICE MASTER 69

Name:
Write the letter and the words.
L $\mathcal{L}$ $\mathcal{L}$ $\mathcal{L}$ $\mathcal{L}$ $\mathcal{L}$ $\mathcal{L}$
$\mathcal{L}$ $\mathcal{L}$ $\mathcal{L}$ $\mathcal{L}$ $\mathcal{L}$ $\mathcal{L}$
Laos   Laredo   Lisbon
Luna   Lloyd   Linus
Write the sentences.
Lee lives near Lima.
Leslie flew to London.
Copyright © Zaner-Bloser, Inc.   Practice Master 69

- Undercurve
- Slant
- Retrace, curve forward and back

Trace and write.

Patty climbed Pike's Peak.
Patty climbed Pike's Peak.

Trace and write.

P is not joined to the letter that follows. Write words that begin with P.

Pennsylvania   Pluto

Write the sentence.

Pike's Peak is so high!

Stroke description to guide letter formation at home:
P Undercurve. Slant. Retrace; curve forward and back.

Slant
Circle a word you wrote that has good slant.

114

Coaching Hint

Evaluating Size To improve poor slant strokes, have students use soft, oversized chalk at the chalkboard, holding it as they would hold a pencil. Place sets of two dots about six inches apart and at the correct slant to mark the starting and stopping points of each slant stroke, and have students connect the dots. (kinesthetic, visual)

1. Present the Letter

Help students focus on the letter **P** by asking:
- Where does **P** begin? (*at the midline*)
- How does **P** begin? (*with an undercurve*)

Model Write **P** on guidelines as you say the stroke description. Model writing **P** in the air as you repeat the stroke description. Have students say the description as they write **P** in the air with you.

Corrective Strategy
The forward oval curves around and goes below the midline.

 not P

2. Write and Evaluate

After students have practiced writing **P** on scrap paper or practice boards, ask them to trace and write the first row of letters.

Stop and Check To help students evaluate **P,** ask:
- Is your **P** about the same width as the model?
- Is your **P** closed?

School to Home

Families may use the stroke description on the student page to encourage good letter formation at home. **Practice Master 107** provides take-home practice for the letters **L** and **P**.

3. Apply

Ask students to complete the page by writing **P** and the words and sentence. Remind students to think about slant as they write, remembering to write their slant strokes parallel.

PRACTICE MASTER 70

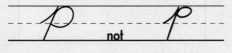

Trace and write.

R R

Rita rides on the Red River.
Rita rides on the Red River.

Trace and write.

R

✓

R is joined to the letter that follows. Write words that begin with *R*.

Rhode Island   Richmond

Write the sentence.

Rita rides the rapids.

 Stroke description to guide letter formation at home:
R Undercurve. Slant. Retrace;
curve forward and back.
Curve forward; undercurve.

Slant
Circle a letter you wrote
that has good slant.

115

- Undercurve
- Slant
- Retrace, curve forward and back
- Curve forward, undercurve

Coaching Hint

Basic Strokes Give each student a card on which one of the basic strokes is written. Tell the student to write that basic stroke on paper and to write all the uppercase and lowercase letters that have that basic stroke. (kinesthetic, visual)

1. Present the Letter

Help students focus on the letter **R** by asking:
- Where does **R** end? *(at the midline)*
- What is the ending stroke? *(undercurve)*

Model Write **R** on guidelines as you say the stroke description. Model writing **R** in the air as you repeat the stroke description. Have students say the words as they use their index finger to write **R** in a layer of shaving cream on their desktop.

Corrective Strategy

Pause at the slant stroke before beginning the second curve forward.

 R not R

2. Write and Evaluate

After students have practiced writing **R** on scrap paper or practice boards, ask them to trace and write the first row of letters.

 Stop and Check To help students evaluate **R,** ask:
- Does your **R** begin at the midline?
- Does your retrace look like a single line?

Families may use the stroke description on the student page to encourage good letter formation at home. **Practice Master 108** provides take-home practice for the letters **R** and **B**.

3. Apply

Ask students to complete the page by writing **R** and the words and sentence. Remind students to think about slant as they write, remembering to make their letters uniform and easy to read.

PRACTICE MASTER 71

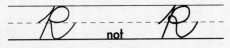

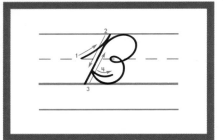

- Undercurve
- Slant
- Retrace, curve forward, loop, curve forward and back
- Retrace, curve right

Coaching Hint

Writing Easily The ability to write letters and words automatically allows students to spend more time thinking about the content of their writing. To make sure students are gaining "automaticity," ask them to demonstrate correct letter formation with their eyes closed. (kinesthetic)

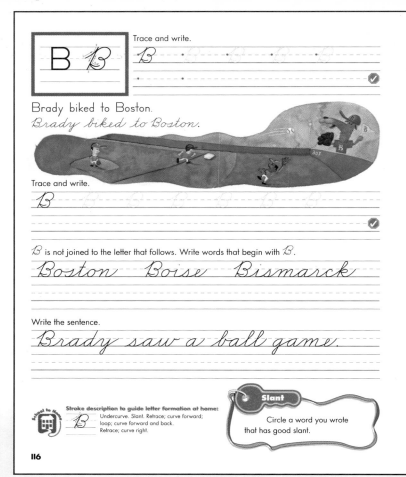

Trace and write.

Brady biked to Boston.
Brady biked to Boston.

Trace and write.

$\mathcal{B}$ is not joined to the letter that follows. Write words that begin with $\mathcal{B}$.

Boston   Boise   Bismarck

Write the sentence.

Brady saw a ball game.

Stroke description to guide letter formation at home:
Undercurve. Slant. Retrace; curve forward;
loop; curve forward and back.
Retrace; curve right.

Slant
Circle a word you wrote that has good slant.

116

---

1 Present the Letter

Help students focus on the letter **B** by asking:
- How are **B** and **R** alike? *(They have the same beginning.)*
- Where does the loop close? *(near the midline)*

Model Write **B** on guidelines as you say the stroke description. Model writing **B** in the air as you repeat the stroke description. Have students say the description as they write **B** in the air with you.

Corrective Strategy

Make sure the ending stroke touches the slant stroke.

2 Write and Evaluate

After students have practiced writing **B** on scrap paper or practice boards, ask them to trace and write the first row of letters.

 Stop and Check To help students evaluate **B,** ask:
- Does your **B** have correct slant?
- Does your **B** rest on the baseline?

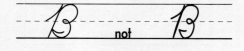

Families may use the stroke description on the student page to encourage good letter formation at home. **Practice Master 108** provides take-home practice for the letters **R** and **B.**

3 Apply

Ask students to complete the page by writing **B** and the words and sentence. Remind students to think about slant as they write, remembering that the letters in legible writing are made with consistent slant.

PRACTICE MASTER 72

TII6

Practice

G S L P R B

Here are some authors whose books you may have read. Write their names.

Brian Pinkney   Jan Brett

Cynthia Rylant   Dr. Seuss

Maurice Sendak

Paul Goble   Lewis Carroll

Eve Bunting   Hugh Lofting

117

Review the Letters

Direct the students to look at the letters being reviewed on student page 117. Ask them what they remember about the shape of these letters. (*All begin with an undercurve-loop or undercurve-slant stroke.*)

Review the stroke descriptions and model again any of the letters the students may be having difficulty writing.

Ask a volunteer to give a verbal description of one of these letters: **G, S, L, P, R, B**. Challenge the other students to identify the letter being described and then write it on guidelines on the chalkboard.

Write and Evaluate

Have the students write the authors' names on student page 117, remembering the Keys to Legibility as they write.

 Stop and Check To help students evaluate their writing, ask:

- Did you write with correct strokes so your letters have proper shape?
- Did you use the guidelines to make letters with correct size?
- Do your short letters touch both the midline and the baseline?
- Do your tall letters touch both the headline and the baseline?
- Do your short letters with descenders touch the headline of the next writing space?
- Did you use good spacing between letters and between words?
- Does your writing have consistent forward slant?

Corrective Strategy

R joins to the letter that follows it.

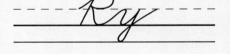

More About Practice

Students who have mastered the skill of writing the lowercase and uppercase letters without models should be given writing activities that will challenge them and require thinking. Reteaching, for any student who still needs it, is most effective if practice is given in the student's dominant learning modality.

Application

Application
Writing About a Book Character

> *I love to read exciting Dr. Doolittle stories. He is a doctor who can talk to the animals. He understands what they say. He helps them feel better.*

Write the paragraph about Dr. Doolittle.

Keys to Legibility

My writing has good shape. ☐
My writing has good size. ☐
My writing has good spacing. ☐
My writing has good slant. ☐

Shape
Size
Spacing
Slant

118

Apply

Review the paragraph about a book character on student page 118. Then have students read and follow the directions. Remind them to write carefully and to remember to follow the Keys to Legibility so their writing will be easy to read.

Help students summarize what they remember about the Keys to Legibility. Then have them respond to the checklist in the Key feature.

Special Helps
Maureen King
Occupational Therapist

Some students may still need help refining dexterity and hand/eye coordination. Set up a work station or provide a folder of supplementary materials, and have students work alone or in small groups to complete activities such as word games and mazes related to the curriculum. Students can use wipe-off transparencies over prepared sheets. Provide a variety of writing implements, and reemphasize such concepts as directionality, retracing carefully in letters such as cursive **t,** and leaving appropriate space between letters, words, and sentences.

Coaching Hint

Teaching Handwriting
Cooperative and collaborative learning create an ideal environment for student interaction. Organize groups so that students of differing strengths join forces to work together. Assist by actively monitoring and advising each group, setting performance time limits, and keeping each team on track.

Review Uppercase Letters

Write these uppercase letters in *cursive*.

A B C D E F G H I

J K L M N O P Q R

S T U V W X Y Z

JOINING ALERT | Remember! These letters are joined to the letter that follows. | *a C E H J K m n R U Y Z*

Write these song titles in *cursive*.

"Kumbaya"

"Yankee Doodle"

"Clementine"

"My Bonnie"

"Are You Sleeping?"

"Home on the Range"

"John Henry"

119

Review Uppercase Letters

Tell students they now have studied and written all of the uppercase cursive letterforms. Guide them in a review of these letters with the following activity.

1. The letters **A, C, E, N, M, K, H, U, Y, Z, J,** and **R** are _____ to the letter that follows. (*joined*)

2. The letters **O, V, X, W, T, F, I, Q, G, S, L, D, P,** and **B** are _____ to the letter that follows. (*not joined*)

3. All uppercase letters are _____ letters. (*tall*)

4. The uppercase letters with descenders are _____. (*J, Y, Z*)

Have students review and practice the basic cursive strokes.

Write the Letters

Encourage students to use their best cursive handwriting as they write the uppercase letters and the song titles on student page 119 and the special days on student page 120. Point out the **Joining Alerts,** and remind students to be aware of which letters are joined to the letter that follows and which are not.

Evaluate

To help students evaluate their writing, ask questions such as these:
• Which of your letters are satisfactory?
• Which of your letters need improvement?
• Which of your joinings are satisfactory?
• Which of your joinings need improvement?

Write the names of special days in *cursive*.

Groundhog Day

Find a Rainbow Day

Thanksgiving

Bird Day

Labor Day

Independence Day

Washington's Birthday

Veterans Day

Pet Owner's Day

Lincoln's Birthday

School Librarian's Day

Dentists' Day

120

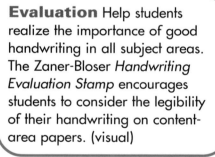

Coaching Hint

Evaluation Help students realize the importance of good handwriting in all subject areas. The Zaner-Bloser *Handwriting Evaluation Stamp* encourages students to consider the legibility of their handwriting on content-area papers. (visual)

Application of Legibility Skills

Students at this level should realize the importance of legibility beyond the daily handwriting lesson. Their skills must be transferred into all areas of the curriculum. An awareness of the importance of handwriting legibility in all subjects will encourage the students to maintain the skills learned. When this awareness is developed, students will have formed good handwriting habits that will stay with them throughout their lives.

Remind students that the four Keys to Legibility all begin with the letter **s** (**shape, size, spacing, and slant**), making them easy to remember. It is hoped that students will eventually perform evaluations mentally, applying the four Keys as a check of the legibility of their writing.

Certificates of Progress *(Practice Master 76) should be awarded to those students who show notable handwriting progress and* **Certificates of Excellence** *(Practice Master 77) to those who progress to the top levels of handwriting ability.*

I'd Like To Be a Lighthouse

I'd like to be a lighthouse
    And scrubbed and painted white.
I'd like to be a lighthouse
    And stay awake all night
To keep my eye on everything
    That sails my patch of sea;
I'd like to be a lighthouse
    With the ships all watching me.

Rachel Field

Write the first four lines of the poem in your best cursive handwriting.

One More Time

Remind students that at the beginning of the school year they wrote this poem as a pretest and evaluated their handwriting. Read the poem aloud with the students. Then point out the writing area on student page 121 where they are to write the poem again. As they write the poem in cursive as a posttest, remind them to use correct letter shape and size, correct spacing, and uniform slant.

Evaluate

Have students use the Keys to Legibility to evaluate their handwriting. Suggest they compare this writing with their writing on the pretest on student page 19, and discuss how their writing has changed. Meet individually with students to help them assess their progress.

Zaner-Bloser's *Evaluation Guide* for grade 3 handwriting is a handy tool for evaluating students' writing. The evaluation criteria are the Keys to Legibility. Samples of children's handwriting, ranging in quality from excellent to poor, provide a helpful comparison for evaluation.

Support for
English-Language Learners
Student Pages 121–127

Comprehension

Posttest, p. TI2I Before you read aloud the poem on student page 121, show pictures of lighthouses. Explain that lighthouses are tall buildings or towers with lights at the top. They are located near the shore of oceans or rivers. Sailors use their lights as navigational aids. The lights also warn of dangers, such as rocks or sandbars.

Beginner/Emergent Speakers: Write the lines of the poem on sentence strips. Tape the strips in the correct order on the board and read them aloud. Then shuffle the strips. Ask volunteers to come to the board and rearrange them in the correct order.

Intermediate Speakers: Create cloze activities to assess students' comprehension of vocabulary. For example, write the lines of the poem on the board, leaving out selected words. You might write, "I'd like to be a _____ / And _____ and painted white." Ask volunteers to fill in the blanks with words from the poem.

Advanced/Fluent Speakers: Have your students create original poems around the theme "I'd like to be a _____." Encourage the use of illustrations and graphic organizers during prewriting. Provide rhyming dictionaries, bilingual dictionaries, and picture dictionaries.

Writing

Narrative Writing, p. TI24 English-Language Learners who have some fluency in English are often reluctant to share their creative writing. These students may use only a limited number of sentence patterns, and they often have problems with sentence structure, organization, word choice, and word order.

Explain that students will work with a writing buddy to write a story about a time when they were surprised. As a student tells his or her story, the writing buddy will record it verbatim. When the writing is complete, the writing buddy will read the story back as the storyteller follows along. The storyteller may then go back and read the story independently.

Manuscript/Cursive The starting and stopping points of manuscript letters usually differ from the starting and stopping points of cursive letters. As you teach proper letter formation, emphasize starting and stopping points.

Vocabulary Development

Homophones, p. TI2I Explain that some English words sound the same but are spelled differently and have different meanings. Use the word *sea* on student page 121 as an example. Help students differentiate the differences in spelling, meaning, and usage of the words *sea* and *see*. Create and label picture cards for *sea* and *see*. Use each word in a sentence to provide context. Then have students write original sentences.

Specific Teaching Tips

The arrangement of words in a sentence varies across language systems. In English, sentences usually appear in an s-v-o (subject-verb-object) construction. In other languages, sentences may be arranged in an s-o-v (subject-object-verb) construction. Pairing English-Language Learners with students who have a strong grasp of the basic conventions of grammar will help them learn to construct sentences properly.

TI22A

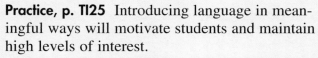
Coaching Hint

Practice, p. T125 Introducing language in meaningful ways will motivate students and maintain high levels of interest.

Beginner/Emergent Speakers: Provide activities that focus on basic skills, such as letter formation, spelling patterns, rules of capitalization and punctuation, and word and sentence order. Appropriate activities include labeling, making lists, and alphabetizing.

Intermediate and Advanced/Fluent Speakers: As their knowledge of English increases, students can begin extended writing tasks. Appropriate activities include writing about a field trip, retelling a story, and creating original stories, poems, and descriptions.

Evaluation

Self-Evaluation, p. T123 Evaluating students' writing and providing corrective strategies will serve various purposes. Identifying errors allows you—and your students—to acknowledge those skills that require additional work. In addition, having students correct their own errors establishes clear standards in spelling and written expression.

Help students develop the skill of self-evaluation by identifying error patterns that will be easy for students to recognize. For example, when reviewing a student's work, you may notice that he or she consistently omits end punctuation. Work with that student to gauge his or her awareness of this error pattern. One way to do this is to have the student read his or her writing aloud to you. If, while reading, the student stops reading when he or she detects an error, that student will more easily incorporate correction strategies than will a student who reads past errors.

Handwriting and the Writing Process

The writing process can be intimidating.

Beginner/Emergent Speakers: Have students complete prewriting activities, such as brainstorming, in their first language. Then, help them create comparable lists of English words and phrases. This strategy prevents language barriers from stifling creativity.

Intermediate and Advanced/Fluent Speakers: Graphic organizers are important tools for organizing ideas and information. Encourage students to create a word web. Model how to transfer words, phrases, and sketches from the web onto individual slips of paper. Students can then arrange and rearrange the papers into meaningful blocks of ideas, sequenced steps, and so on. This activity gives students direction and provides them with words to use in their writing.

Writing Quickly, p. T122 For students whose first language does not use the Roman alphabet, the time required for achieving handwriting fluency may be longer than that needed by students who have more familiarity with Roman letters and numerals. Writing exercises help students gain proficiency and fluency in handwriting. They also reinforce the left-to-right progression of letters and words and provide practice with vocabulary, spelling, word order, and punctuation.

Beginner/Emergent Speakers: Have students practice writing letters, students' names, and the names of common objects.

Intermediate/Fluent Speakers: Encourage students to write stories, poems, song lyrics, and other meaningful text.

CULTURAL NOTES

Writing requires the use of many cognitive functions. For this reason, many students may have difficulty simultaneously processing vocabulary, sentence structure, spelling, and proper letter formation. During each writing activity, have students focus specifically on only one or two of these writing conventions.

Using Cursive Writing

Writing Quickly

The goal of handwriting instruction is to enable students to write legibly with ease and fluency. It is important, however, not to stress fluency (speed) too early. Students should master writing the lowercase and uppercase alphabets before there is a concern for speed. By the end of third grade, students should be able to write legibly, without stress, approximately 40 letters per minute. Based on this estimate, the students should be able to write the saying on the page, legibly and without stress, in about one minute and fifteen seconds.

Why Write Quickly?

Discuss with the students times when being able to write quickly might be helpful or necessary. These might include writing a note in class, copying an address or telephone number from TV, jotting down ideas as they come to mind, writing words for a spelling test, and writing a story. Emphasize the importance of maintaining legibility even when writing quickly. Describe a time when you or someone you know wrote important information quickly—and were unable to read it later.

Coaching Hint

Automaticity The ability to write letters and words automatically allows students to spend more time thinking about the content of their writing. To make sure students are gaining automaticity, ask them to demonstrate correct letter formation with their eyes closed. (visual, kinesthetic)

Writing Quickly

Writing quickly is a skill that will help when you need to write a story, take a timed test, or take notes.

Writing that is done quickly should still be easy to read. With practice, you will learn how to make your writing speedy and legible.

Read the saying. Write it quickly and legibly.

In fourteen hundred ninety-two Columbus sailed the ocean blue.

Now write the lines again.
Try to write them faster this time.

Write and Evaluate

Direct the students to look at the saying on the page and to read it with you. Review any letters that still present difficulties for any of the students. When the students seem comfortable with the task, have them write the saying the first time, trying to write more quickly than usual but still writing letters that are easy to read.

Note: If you want to make this an actual timed writing, have the students begin at your signal. After exactly one minute, have the students stop and put a mark, such as a star or a checkmark, after the letter they just completed. Then have them finish the saying.

Count the letters in each student's marked passage. Most third-graders can be expected to write about 40 letters legibly in one minute. Then have them write the saying a second time. Repeat the timed writing procedure, if you want.

After the children write, encourage them to evaluate their letters and words by comparing them to the models. Ask questions such as these:

• Do your letters have good shape?
• Do your tall letters touch the headline?
• Do your short letters touch the midline?
• Do **f** and **y** go below the baseline and touch the next headline?
• Do your words have good letter spacing?
• Is there good spacing between your words?
• Does your writing have consistent forward slant?

Write the saying two more times.
Try to write it even faster, but keep it easy to read.

_____

_____

_____

_____

_____

_____

_____

Now read your final writing. Circle Yes or No to respond to each statement. Then show your writing to another reader, either a classmate or your teacher. Ask that person to circle Yes or No beside each statement.

	My Evaluation	My Classmate's or Teacher's Evaluation
The writing is easy to read.	Yes No	Yes No
The writing has good Shape.	Yes No	Yes No
The writing has good Size.	Yes No	Yes No
The writing has good Spacing.	Yes No	Yes No
The writing has good Slant.	Yes No	Yes No

123

Writing More Quickly

Direct the students to look at the writing space on page 123 in their books. Point out that this space is where they are to write the saying two more times. Encourage the students to try to write faster than they did during the other two times, but caution them not to sacrifice legibility for the sake of speed.

For timed writing, follow the procedure recommended earlier in this lesson. Help the students evaluate their writing by comparing it to the models and to their previous attempts in this lesson. Then have them respond to the evaluation checklist on the student page.

Note: It is suggested that you have the students write the saying twice in one handwriting lesson and again during the next handwriting lesson. This should prevent the students from tiring and enable them to continue to write well and not feel stressed.

Evaluation

Self-evaluation is an important step in the handwriting process. By identifying their own handwriting strengths and weaknesses, students become independent learners. The steps in their self-evaluation process are as follows:

1. Question

Students should ask themselves questions such as these: "Is my slant correct?" "Do my letters rest on the baseline?"

2. Compare

Students should compare their handwriting to correct models.

3. Evaluate

Students should determine strengths and weaknesses in their handwriting based on the Keys to Legibility.

4. Diagnose

Students should diagnose the cause of any difficulties. Possible causes include incorrect paper or pencil position, inconsistent pressure on pencil, and incorrect strokes.

5. Improve

Self-evaluation should include a means of improvement through additional instruction and continued practice.

Writing Easily

Now that students have been introduced to the formation of all the cursive letters, they can begin to increase the ease with which they write. The ability to write letters and words automatically allows students to spend more time thinking about the content of their writing.

Writing Easily

As you write stories and essays for school papers and tests, it is important that your handwriting flows easily. When you automatically know how to write legibly, you don't have to worry about your handwriting. You are free to think about what you want your writing to say. With practice, you will learn how to make your writing easy, quick, and legible.

Read the writing prompt below. Respond to it by writing on the lines. Let your handwriting flow easily as you think and write.

Narrative Writing

Think about a time when you were surprised by someone or something.

Write a story telling about what happened when you were surprised. Include details to make your writing interesting.

Present the Activity

Direct the students to the writing prompt and the related illustration on student page 124. Encourage discussion about the specific genre being used (narrative writing), and have volunteers name and describe the writing process steps to help them begin planning their writing. (You may want to refer to page T126.) Then have them respond to the prompt on the page by writing a story about a time when they were surprised.

Now read your writing. Circle Yes or No to respond to each statement. Then show your writing to another reader, either a classmate or your teacher. Ask that person to circle Yes or No beside each statement.

	My Evaluation	My Classmate's or Teacher's Evaluation
The writing is easy to read.	Yes No	Yes No
The writing has good (Shape).	Yes No	Yes No
The writing has good (Size).	Yes No	Yes No
The writing has good (Spacing).	Yes No	Yes No
The writing has good (Slant).	Yes No	Yes No

125

Evaluate

On student page 125, point out the evaluation guide. Read the statements with the students, and encourage them to evaluate their writing and respond to the evaluation comments. Then have them refer to a classmate or to the teacher for additional evaluation.

Coaching Hint

Practice To reinforce both cursive and manuscript writing, have the students do many different kinds of writing. Activities may include the following:

- Label pictures and objects.
- Make lists of things in categories.
- Write about field trips.
- Write facts.
- Retell a story in writing.
- Write about books.
- Write stories, poems, and descriptions.
- Write the names of friends and pets.
- Prepare invitations to parties.
- List games for parties.
- Send holiday greetings to parents and friends.

Handwriting and the Writing Process

As students participate in the writing process, let them know that good handwriting is always important. Notes, webs, story drafts, and published pieces that are easy to read cut down on confusion in the classroom. They also help students express their ideas clearly and confidently.

Review with the students the five steps in the writing process identified on student page 126. Encourage discussion on the use-fulness of each step as students develop their writing.

Handwriting and the Writing Process
Write a Paragraph

A paragraph is a group of sentences about one subject. Write a paragraph about your school.

1. Prewriting
Prewriting means gathering ideas and planning before you write. List your ideas on a piece of paper. Then plan your paragraph, telling the subject and in what order you will write your ideas.

2. Drafting
Drafting means putting your thoughts into written sentences for the first time. Use the ideas you listed in Prewriting to draft your paragraph. Write your first draft.

3. Revising
Revising means changing your writing to make it say exactly what you mean. Read your draft. Mark any changes you want to make.

Does your writing include all the information readers want to know?   Yes   No

4. Editing
Editing means checking your revised writing for errors in spelling, punctuation, capitalization, and handwriting.

Are all words spelled correctly?	Yes No
Have you used uppercase letters and punctuation correctly?	Yes No
Do your letters have good shape and size?	Yes No
Does your writing have good spacing?	Yes No
Does your writing have good slant?	Yes No
Is your writing easy to read?	Yes No

5. Publishing
Publishing means using your best handwriting to make a good copy of your writing. Share your writing with others.

126

Prewriting
What should I write?
During prewriting, students plan for their writing by making notes, lists, and webs. Carelessly written prewriting work may cause confusion throughout the writing process, but easy-to-read notes and webs smooth the way for students, teachers, and writing partners.

Drafting
I write my ideas in sentences.
Students' best handwriting isn't necessary for a first draft. In fact, concentrating on handwriting may take students' attention away from the content of their writing. However, a "sloppy" draft makes revising and editing more difficult. As students develop a conscious-ness about legibility, their writing will be fluent **and** easy to read.

Revising
What should I change?
As students revise their drafts, remind them to begin each sen-tence with an uppercase letter and to use an end mark. The revising stage is also a good time to check slant and spacing in the writing. As they revise, students should continue to be aware of the need for legibility.

Editing
How can I improve my spelling and handwriting?
To complete the writing process, have the students edit their drafts, checking spelling, punctuation, and handwriting. Thinking about legibility should always be part of the editing stage of the writing process. The Keys to Legibility— shape, size, spacing, slant—help students know what to look for.

Publishing
How will I share my work?
When publishing writing, it's especially important for students to use their best handwriting. Neat, legible writing shows courtesy to readers. It makes a good first impression, and it helps ensure that readers will understand the writer's message.

Record of Student's Handwriting Skills

Cursive

	Needs Improvement	Shows Mastery		Needs Improvement	Shows Mastery
Sits correctly	☐	☐	Writes the undercurve to undercurve joining	☐	☐
Positions paper correctly	☐	☐	Writes the undercurve to downcurve joining	☐	☐
Holds pencil correctly	☐	☐	Writes the undercurve to overcurve joining	☐	☐
Writes undercurve strokes	☐	☐	Writes the checkstroke to undercurve joining	☐	☐
Writes downcurve strokes	☐	☐	Writes the checkstroke to downcurve joining	☐	☐
Writes overcurve strokes	☐	☐	Writes the checkstroke to overcurve joining	☐	☐
Writes slant strokes	☐	☐	Writes the overcurve to undercurve joining	☐	☐
Writes **i, t, u, w**	☐	☐	Writes the overcurve to downcurve joining	☐	☐
Writes **e, l, b, h, f, k**	☐	☐	Writes the overcurve to overcurve joining	☐	☐
Writes **r, s, j, p**	☐	☐			
Writes **a, d, g, o, c, q**	☐	☐			
Writes numerals **1–10**	☐	☐			
Writes **n, m, y, x, v, z**	☐	☐			
Writes **A, O, D, C, E**	☐	☐	Writes with correct shape	☐	☐
Writes **N, M, H, K**	☐	☐	Writes with correct size	☐	☐
Writes **U, Y, Z**	☐	☐	Writes with correct spacing	☐	☐
Writes **V, W, X**	☐	☐	Writes with correct slant	☐	☐
Writes **I, J, Q**	☐	☐	Regularly checks written work for legibility	☐	☐
Writes **T, F**	☐	☐			
Writes **G, S, L**	☐	☐			
Writes **P, R, B**	☐	☐			

127

The **Record of Student's Handwriting Skills** serves to indicate each student's progress in mastering the skills presented. The chart lists the essential skills in the program. After the skills that are listed have been practiced and evaluated, you will be able to mark the **Record of Student's Handwriting Skills** for either *Shows Mastery* or *Needs Improvement*.

Needs Improvement

If a student has not mastered a skill, provide additional basic instruction and practice. First, determine the student's specific needs. Then return to the initial teaching steps of the lesson for ways to help the student. To improve letterforms, have the student practice writing the letter in isolation and within words and sentences. Reinforce instruction through activities geared to the student's modality strengths. Ask the student to evaluate his or her writing with you. Reevaluate the student's writing following practice over time. When mastery of the skill is achieved, check *Shows Mastery*.

Note: *The* **Record of Student's Handwriting Skills** *is reproduced on* **Practice Master 75**.

Shows Mastery

Mastery of written letterforms is achieved when the student writes the letters using correct basic strokes. Compare the student's written letterforms with the letter models shown in the book. Keep in mind the Keys to Legibility (shape, size, spacing, slant) when evaluating letters, numerals, punctuation marks, words, and sentences for mastery of skill. Observation will indicate whether a student has mastered such skills as pencil and paper positions.

Check the appropriate box for each skill.

Index

APPENDIX
English-Language Learners

The number of English-Language Learners (ELL)—students whose primary or dominant language is one other than English—in American classrooms continues to climb. The diversity and richness that these students add to the classroom does not come without cost. Differences in language, cultural backgrounds, literacy skills, and school experiences can make instruction a challenge for classroom teachers.

ELL students come to school with a wide range of experiences and abilities. Some will be as well schooled as their native-English-speaking peers, while others may have had little, if any, formal schooling. Some will show a facility for learning a new language while others may show more modest progress in their language acquisition. Some will want to embrace culture in the United States, while others will be more reluctant. It is important to keep in mind that ELL students are as diverse in their wants, needs, and abilities as their native-English-speaking peers.

Being aware of cross-cultural differences can make planning for instruction more effective and can help your students be more successful in the mastery of the linguistic components of language.

Cultural Differences

Developing an awareness of cultural diversity is essential when teaching students of diverse backgrounds.

Terms of Address

In the United States, students most often address their teachers with a title, such as Ms., Mr., Miss, or Mrs., and a last name. Teachers most often address students by their first names. In Latin American and Asian schools, students address their teachers as "teacher" (*Maestro* or *Maestra* or *Sensei*), and teachers address their students by their family names. In Israeli schools, both students and teachers address one another by their first names. Depending on students' prior school experiences, they may not immediately respond when called by their first name. In fact, some students may initially be surprised or even offended to be called by their first name at school.

Gender Issues

Some of your students may come from countries in which education is reserved predominantly for males. Cultural norms in these countries may prohibit women from speaking in front of a group of males unless they are first addressed. Consequently, female students may believe it is inappropriate to participate in discussions in a class in which there is a mix of boys and girls. Some male students may find it difficult to view female students as equals. Some may also find it difficult to relate to female teachers, as they may not be used to women being in positions of authority.

Proxemics

Every culture has its own comfort zone (or zones) regarding how close or far apart people stand as they interact. Americans feel most comfortable when there is about four feet between people in social situations. People from high-contact cultures, such as Latin or Mediterranean cultures, are comfortable with less distance. People from low-contact cultures, such as those in Northern Europe or Asian cultures, often prefer more space. When an individual crosses cultural boundaries, tension surfaces and can make both the speaker and receiver uncomfortable.

Body Language

Differences in nonverbal communication abound across cultures and can create confusion and misunderstanding for ELL students. For example, it is a sign of respect in mainstream American culture for a student to make eye contact with the teacher. However, in some cultures (including Native American), establishing eye contact with the teacher is considered a sign of disrespect. Smiling may be perceived as being forward or brazen. Gestures viewed as positive or friendly in one culture may be viewed as hostile or inappropriate in another.

Academic Skills

Some ELL students will have a very rich academic history with well-developed literacy skills and content knowledge comparable to those of their native-English-speaking peers. Others may have little or inconsistent formal schooling and underdeveloped literacy skills in their primary or dominant language. Research has found that students who are literate in their dominant language tend to develop literacy skills in a second language more readily than do students who have not yet developed these skills in their dominant language.

Differences in Classroom Expectations

American classrooms tend to be more interactive than those in many other countries. Students are expected to participate in class discussions, work with partners or in groups, and use manipulatives or other learning tools. ELL students may feel uncomfortable participating in hands-on learning activities or group discussions. They may not take the use of manipulatives seriously.

Feedback

American teachers may demonstrate approval or show praise publicly, pointing out a student's achievement or accomplishment. In some cultures, such overt demonstrations may be viewed as embarrassing to the student or inappropriately boastful.

School-to-Home Issues

American classrooms have long had a tradition of parental involvement in both class-room activities and homework. Parents are expected to reinforce classroom learning at home, work with teachers to prevent potential problems, and even question teachers about their children's curriculum. This tradition may be foreign to the parents of ELL students, who often see a more distinct delineation between the responsibility of the school and the home. Parental involvement could be seen as confrontational or disrespectful. As a result, parents of ELL students may rarely respond to requests for volunteerism or school social events. This cultural difference can sometimes be interpreted as parents' indifference or disinterest in their children's schooling.

Additionally, a parent's own limited English proficiency may inhibit his or her involvement in school life. Here are some suggestions for fostering relationships and encouraging parent participation.

Find a Common Language

Without a common language, very little communication can occur. Find out what the preferred language of the parents of your ELL students is. Translate notes and other communication into the parents' preferred languages when possible. When holding conferences, provide adult translators when possible. This will allow parents to better track their child's progress and will keep them informed about school events and policies.

Make Parents Aware of Resources and Learning Opportunities

Empower parents by making them aware of available community resources. Provide a list of bilingual staff within your school and resource specialists within your school district. Parents may feel more comfortable approaching people who can speak their dominant language.

Educate Parents

Parents will be unfamiliar with how schools operate in the United States. Take them on a tour of the school. Explain the curriculum in a language they can understand. Discuss school and classroom rules, expectations, and the purpose and function of governing bodies and parent organizations.

Celebrate Culture and Heritage

Learn more about the countries and cultures of your ELL students. Provide opportunities for students and parents to share their experiences and culture. Parents may be even more limited in English-language proficiency than their children. Encouraging parents to maintain and share their language and heritage can boost self-esteem and deepen the school-to-home connection.

Teacher Resources

Books

Bouchard, Margaret T. *Comprehension Strategies for English Language Learners.* Scholastic, 2005.

> Margaret Bouchard offers techniques for presenting material that improves comprehension in content classrooms.

Gibbons, Pauline. *Scaffolding Language, Scaffolding Learning: Teaching Second Language Learners in the Mainstream Classroom.* Heinemann, 2002.

> Gibbons presents tips for classroom instruction to teachers with little or no specialized ELL training.

Herrell, Adrienne L. and Michael L. Jordan. *Fifty Strategies for Teaching English Language Learners.* Prentice Hall, 2003.

> Herrell and Jordan offer teachers strategies that support TESOL (Teachers of English to Speakers of Other Languages) goals and standards and are designed to increase students' understanding of content across the curriculum. The authors define, rationalize, and offer step-by-step instructions for the strategies they present.

Peregoy, Suzanne F. and Owen F. Boyle. *Reading, Writing, and Learning in ESL: A Resource Book for K–12 Teachers.* Allyn and Bacon, 2000.

> Peregoy and Boyle examine practices and theories in ELL education. They present teaching and assessment strategies, address socio-cultural issues that can affect classroom instruction, and provide a comprehensive bibliography of resources ELL teachers can use for additional help and research.

Web Resources

NCELA: National Clearinghouse for English Language Acquisition Online Library

This Web site provides practical resources, articles, and other publications directed at educating culturally diverse students.
http://www.ncela.gwu.edu

NCTE: The National Council of Teachers of English

This Web site provides access to contemporary teaching strategies, professional articles addressing issues in bilingual education, and related ELL resources.

http://www.ncte.org/collections/elemell

NEA: National Education Association

This Web site provides curriculum support for ELL teachers.

http://www.nea.org/neatodayextra/ell.html

The following NEA link takes teachers to a list of web resources for ELL teachers, administrators, parents, and students. This list also includes links to national organizations offering intercultural support.

http://www.nea.org/neatodayextra/ellwebresources.html

Teacher Notes

Teacher Notes

Teacher Notes

Teacher Notes